THE WAR
IN PICTURES

THIRD YEAR

ODHAMS PRESS LIMITED

LONG ACRE, LONDON, W. C. 2

Tanks leaving a British port on the first stage of their journey to the Russian front.

THE RUSSIAN GLORY

WHEN Hitler launched his legions against the unknown might of the Soviet Union on 22 June, 1941, several political events that had mystified the world during the two preceding years at once became clear. The Russo-German pact of 23 August, 1939, for example, could now be viewed in its proper perspective; Russia's occupation of Polish territory after the German attack on that country was explained, as were also the incorporation of the Baltic States within the Soviet Union and Russia's demand for and occupation of the Rumanian territories of Bessarabia and Bukovina. The reasons for the drastic purges in the Russian Army and for the attack upon Finland, too, became plain in the light of the German attack on Russia, and fitted in with the other events to complete the jigsaw.

Hitler had been playing the game he had played so often before. With treaties of friendship and pacts of non-aggression he had tried to lull the suspicions of his powerful eastern neighbour until, having completed his conquests in the west, he could switch the whole of his armed might eastwards and remove the last barrier that stood between him and his dream of European domination. But in Stalin, the Soviet dictator, Hitler had met a man who could match cunning with cunning —a man who, in this great game of political poker, was his equal at least, if not his master.

When Germany offered to sign a pact of non-aggression with the Soviet Union in 1939, therefore, Stalin readily accepted. He knew that Europe was on the brink of war, but he knew, too, that Germany did not want to be involved in a war on two fronts at the same time and that he could expect a year's, or perhaps two years' respite during which he could build up his forces and reinforce his frontiers against the clash which he recognized as inevitable. So when Germany marched into Poland from the west, Stalin marched in from the east and by the subsequent division of that unhappy country on 29 September, 1939, he forged the first link in the chain of buffer states that was to protect his western frontier from the Baltic to the Black Sea.

3

GERMAN ADVANCE IN SOUTHERN POLAND. The German drive towards Kiev was made by way of Lwow and Luck, which fell on 30 June and 1 July respectively, after fierce air and tank battles. The dreadful destruction wrought in these battles is shown by this aerial picture of Luck, taken after the Germans had passed.

Stalin's next move came in November, 1939, when he made territorial demands on Finland, and when these were refused, took what he wanted by force of arms. The war dragged on until 12 March, 1940, and the Finns put up a magnificent resistance, but in the end they were forced to cede the whole of the Karelian Isthmus, an area in central Finland and the Rybachi Peninsula in the north. In this way Stalin was able to protect three vital areas—Leningrad, the railway to Murmansk and Murmansk itself—from possible attack from the west.

THE BUFFER STATES

In June, whilst Hitler's forces were still tied up in the west, reorganizing after their lightning push through France and the Low Countries, Russia demanded Bessarabia and Bukovina from Rumania and occupied these areas on the 28th, and in the following month, when Latvia, Estonia and Lithuania decided to become Soviet republics the last link in the chain was added. The pre-war western frontier of the U.S.S.R. was now well buffered for its whole length against any attempt at encroachment upon Russia proper.

Stalin had timed these moves with consummate skill. Hitler's hands were full, and Stalin knew it, and it was not until after the German plans for invading Britain had come to nought that the German dictator was able to turn his attention to other theatres.

Meanwhile, Hitler's ally, Italy, was getting herself into difficulties. In Libya and in East Africa her armies were in full retreat whilst her much heralded invasion of Greece had resolved itself into a not very successful defence of Albania.

By the end of April, Germany was ready to take a hand once again in the war in Europe. She began by forcing Bulgaria to join the Axis and a similar attempt to persuade Yugoslavia to do the same was foiled only by a revolution in that country. As a result Germany invaded Yugoslavia on 6 April, and on the same day Nazi troops crossed the frontier into Greece. By the 17th Yugoslavia was forced to capitulate, but Greece, with the support of British and Empire troops, carried on the fight until 30 April when the British troops were obliged to evacuate that country. On 20 May Hitler followed up his successes with an airborne attack on Crete and within ten days had gained complete control of the island and forced the British to carry out yet another evacuation.

Meanwhile, in Africa, the Germans, taking full advantage of the withdrawal of British and Empire troops for service in Greece, had launched an attack upon the small forces left to guard Cyrenaica. All the territory taken from the Italians by the Army of the Nile was recovered by General Rommel, commander of the Afrika Korps, leaving only Tobruk in British hands.

Hitler now put pressure on the Vichy Government of France with a view to gaining control of Syria, and Axis aircraft actually began using Syrian airfields and flying war materials to that country by air from Crete. Had he achieved his purpose German arms would have constituted a grave threat to Suez, both from Cyrenaica and Syria, and in addition would have succeeded in getting uncomfortably close to the Russian oilfields in the Caucasus. British troops, however, entered Syria and fighting broke out between British and Vichy French troops. It was while this fighting was going on that the world was startled by the news of the German onslaught on Soviet Russia.

HITLER'S CHOICE

Hitler's invasion of the Soviet Union came as a surprise to many people, yet it was the logical course of events. Hitler, in fact, had only two courses left open to him: he must attack either

GERMANS STORM RUSSIAN STRONG POINT. The mechanized spearheads of the German attacks frequently penetrated far in advance of their supporting troops, leaving pockets of resistance in their rear. These were mopped up by the infantry, but so stubbornly did the Russians hold their ground that it was sometimes days before their resistance could be overcome. Above: German soldiers are seen cautiously approaching a Russian blockhouse with hand grenades during mopping-up operations on the northern front.

Invasion of Russia

Great Britain or Russia. The whole of Europe from the English Channel to the Black Sea was now in his hands or under his control. After his attempt to outflank Turkey via Syria had failed, Hitler could expand no further without encroaching upon the preserves of his eastern neighbour or violating the sovereignty of Turkey itself. This would obviously have been likely to have caused friction with Russia owing to the strategic importance of the Dardanelles and might even have brought Turkey into the war on Russia's side thereby dangerously exposing the right flank oi the German armies.

Hitler therefore chose the Soviet Union as his next victim. An all-out invasion of Britain with the armed might of Russia at his back door was not the sort of enterprise to appeal to a man of Hitler's mentality. He knew that he, at any rate, never intended to keep his promises to Russia and strongly suspected that Russia knew it too.

Hitler, in his declaration to the German people just after his troops crossed the Soviet frontier, admitted that the presence of large Russian forces near the frontier was causing him anxiety. "While our soldiers from 10 May onwards were breaking the power of Britain and France in the west," he said, "the Russian military deployment on our eastern frontier was being continued to a more and more menacing extent. From August, 1940, onwards I therefore considered it to be in the interests of the Reich no longer to permit our eastern provinces . . . to remain unprotected in the face of this tremendous concentration of Bolshevist divisions. Thus came about the result intended by the British and Russian co-operation —namely, the tying up of such powerful German forces in the east that the radical conclusion of the war in the west, particularly as regards aircraft, could no longer be vouched for by the German High Command."

By moving east Hitler undoubtedly took what he thought to be the safer course. The English Channel, which had stood as an effective barrier to his invasion of Britain would serve to protect his back whilst his armies were engaged on the eastern front.

ATTITUDE OF BRITAIN AND U.S.

Moreover, he hoped that by bringing Russia into the conflict he would create a division of aim and of effort in the democracies, particularly in the U.S.A., which would be of considerable advantage to him. Indeed, the outbreak of Russo-German hostilities led to a fresh outburst by the American isolationists, who demanded that the United States should stay out of the war and refrain from giving aid to Russia.

But Hitler's mind was soon disillusioned, first of all by Mr. Churchill, who declared that any state that fought against Nazism would receive British aid and later by Mr. Sumner Welles, U.S. Under Secretary of State, who said that in the opinion of the American Government any defence against Hitlerism or any rallying of the forces opposing Hitlerism, from whatsoever source they might spring, would hasten the downfall of the present German leaders and would, therefore, redound to the benefit of American defence and security as a whole.

HITLER'S OBJECTIVE

The invasion of Russia started at 4 a.m. on the morning of 22 June, 1941, and fierce fighting broke out along the whole of the 1,800 mile frontier from the Baltic to the Black Sea. The invasion resolved itself into four main thrusts: 1, through the Baltic States towards Leningrad; 2, in Central Poland in the direction of Minsk and Moscow; 3, in Southern Poland towards Lwow, with Kiev as its objective; and 4, in Bessarabia towards Odessa.

If Hitler thought that his soldiers would win an easy victory, he was soon to be disappointed. Everywhere the invaders were met and resisted with courage and determination by the Red Army and Air Force, and it soon became apparent that the Russian commanders had learned the lessons from the German campaigns in Poland and France and that in the tactical handling of their forces they were only a very little inferior to the Germans.

The whole success of the German plan of campaign lay in speed. Hitler hoped that by a rapid capture of Moscow and Leningrad, he would undermine Russian morale to such an extent that they would cease to offer effective resistance, for Leningrad, the cradle of the revolution, held a special significance in Russian minds, besides being the key to the Baltic, whilst Moscow was the hub of all Russian communications and the centre of government. It was even said that the German High Command were confident that they would roll the Russians back to a line Archangel-Astrakhan before winter set in, thereby cutting Russia off from all possible outside aid and, at the same time, gaining control of the valuable industrial and mineral resources upon which Russia relied for the prosecution of the war. This ambitious plan would have to be carried out in something like twelve weeks before the Russian winter closed down upon the antagonists and restricted further large-scale operations.

Yet after two weeks of war the Nazis had scarcely penetrated Russian territory proper. True, they had occupied practically the whole of

sectors the Red armies were holding well and were taking a terrible toll of the invaders by well-timed counter-attacks. In all this fighting the Red Air Force played a prominent part, giving excellent support to the ground forces as well as carrying out raids on vital enemy objectives behind the lines.

GERMAN ANTI-TANK GUNNERS IN ACTION. The war on the Eastern front was remarkable for the great tank battles that developed between rival forces. These vehicles were so strongly protected by armour-plate that special anti-tank guns were required to deal with them. The anti-tank gunners seen above are using a wooden stake palisade as cover as they await the coming of Russian tanks reported in the neighbourhood.

Poland and the Baltic States, with the exception of Estonia, but the speed of their advance must have fallen far short of their expectations. Thus, the buffer states fulfilled Stalin's object and held the enemy at bay long enough to allow the High Command to dispose its forces to the best advantage.

The greatest threat to the Russians was the German drive into White Russia where Minsk, the capital, fell on 30 June, but in the other

During the next two weeks the main German strength was directed in the north through Estonia and Latvia towards Narva and Ostrov, these two towns forming the two arms of a pincer movement towards Leningrad. In the central sector a penetration of the Russian lines towards Vitebsk constituted a direct threat to Smolensk, whilst further south a similar penetration towards Zhitomir brought the enemy within sixty miles of Kiev, capital of the Ukraine. In Bessarabia the

SMOLENSK IN FLAMES. The town of Smolensk fell into German hands on 13 August after some of the fiercest fighting of the war. Its loss was a serious blow to the Russians, for it brought the enemy considerably closer to the capital. Here, as everywhere else, the Russians carried out the "scorched earth" policy with the greatest thoroughness, blowing up military stores and destroying everything that could help the enemy. The blazing buildings seen above were set on fire by the defenders before they evacuated the town.

thrust towards Odessa was successfully held and only slight progress was made.

During these operations the Germans made fantastic claims for their arms. On 12 July, for example, the German High Command in a special communique spoke as if the war was almost over. The fall of Leningrad and Kiev, it said, was imminent; there were increasing signs of disintegration in the Russian units; the road to Moscow lay open; final German victory was now assured beyond all doubt.

HEAVY GERMAN LOSSES

It cannot be disputed that the German advances during this period were considerable, but the spearhead of their attack was frequently many miles ahead of the supporting troops, and the activities of the Soviet guerrilla bands in the rear of the enemy lines were tying up large bodies of soldiers who should have been following up the

motorized divisions. Moreover, there can be little doubt that these advances were made at tremendous cost to the attackers and that as the advance deepened an almost superhuman burden was placed upon the ever lengthening and constantly threatened lines of communication.

Thus on 19 July the first phase of the battle came to a close, and for the next fortnight the front remained almost static. This breathing space allowed the Germans to rest their tired troops, bring up reserves, consolidate the positions they had won, and repair their damaged tanks and aeroplanes.

There were, however, three small but important advances during this period. In the north the towns of Pskov and Ostrov were taken; on the central front the Vitebsk salient was deepened after severe fighting along the Upper Dnieper as far as the outskirts of Smolensk and in the south, where the Zhitomir wedge was widened and the towns of Korosten, Berdichev and Byela Tserkov were captured. This last advance, though small in itself, brought the enemy dangerously close to the gates of Kiev.

By early August the Germans had regrouped their forces and were ready to take the offensive once more. The advance on Leningrad was renewed with unprecedented ferocity. The forces commanded by von Leeb, supported by masses of aircraft, blasted their way to Luga and Novgorod, which fell on 25 August. From there, after only a short pause a further advance brought about the fall of Tallinn. The whole of Estonia was now in German hands. Leningrad was almost encircled and only the most stubborn defence by the Russians kept the invaders in check. This great battle was described by a Russian spokesman as "an immense and bloody battle that continued day and night," but though the German pressure continued unabated until the middle of September they failed to take the city, although, by capturing Schlüsselburg, twenty-five miles to the east, on 7 September, they completed its encirclement.

On the central front equally notable advances were made. Smolensk fell on 11 August to be followed quickly by Mogilev, Gomel and Chernigov. The Germans thereby straightened out their line and constituted a new threat to Kiev from the north.

RETREAT TO THE DNIEPER

But it was in the Ukraine that the most spectacular advances were made. Here the Germans suddenly switched their attack from Byela Tserkov, south-eastwards in the direction of Uman, thereby turning the whole of the Russian defences on the rivers Dniester and Bug and forcing Marshal Budenny's armies to retreat to the line of the River Dnieper.

Only with the greatest difficulty did Marshal Budenny manage to elude the rapidly closing ring which von Runstedt had thrown around his armies, but in spite of very heavy losses the major

THE RAVAGES OF WAR. Many fine Russian towns were reduced to a mass of charred and twisted ruins during the German advances in Russia. Blasted by attack from the air and by siege artillery, they were, nevertheless, held to the last and evacuated only when all hope of holding them had gone. This ruined street is typical of the scenes of desolation that greeted the Germans on their "triumphant" entry into a captured town.

BEHIND THE ENEMY LINES. A feature of the campaign in Russia was the activity of guerrilla bands which operated far behind the enemy lines and wrought havoc with his communications. These hardy warriors, some of whom are seen above, worked mainly at night, blowing up railway lines, mining roads and carrying out lightning attacks on isolated bodies of enemy troops. Their activities had a most demoralizing effect on the German soldiers who went in constant fear of swift and unexpected attack from these fierce and stealthy fighters.

portion of the Russian forces managed to withdraw in time to evade annihilation.

For the moment the Russians were on the run, and the Germans were quick to follow up this advantage. Kremenchug fell on 14 September and the enemy thereby gained a valuable bridgehead across the Dnieper. Moreover, with Chernigov lost, Kiev was now at the apex of a dangerous salient, being threatened both from north and south.

CROSSING OF THE DNIEPER

This precipitate retreat cost the Russians dear. The important iron-ore town of Krivoi Rog was lost; they had been forced to destroy the great Dnieper Dam at Zaporozhe which had been built under the first Five-year Plan; and they had been deprived of the port of Nikolayev with its shipbuilding yards and other important industries. Odessa was now completely encircled but continued to hold out.

During the second half of September activity on the north and central fronts died down. Only in the Ukraine did the German advance continue.

The pincers threatening Kiev were closed and on 19 September the town had to be evacuated. Once again the Russian armies escaped encirclement in the nick of time.

In the extreme south the Germans succeeded in accomplishing one of the most remarkable feats of the war—the crossing of the Dnieper—and capturing Perekop and Kherson. The Crimea was now isolated and a dangerous threat to the Caucasus was developing.

During these fateful days, when the Nazi flood was rushing inexorably eastwards, the Russians never for a moment wavered or lost their cohesion. They displayed a remarkable aptitude as tank and aeroplane fighters, and took huge toll of enemy aircraft and armoured vehicles. Moreover, they carried out the "scorched earth policy" to the full, and before evacuating their towns systematically destroyed everything that could be of any possible use to the enemy.

Whilst these events were taking place on the eastern front, Britain was doing all in her power to assist her hard-pressed ally. On 15 September Lord Beaverbrook announced that all tanks made in Britain during the week 22 to 29 September, would be sent to Russia, and on the 29th the Moscow Three-Power Conference between Britain, U.S.A. and Russia met to examine requirements from Britain and the U.S.A. necessary to the supply of the Soviet Union. Lord Beaverbrook and Mr. Averell Harriman, leaders of the British and American Missions, met M. Stalin and M. Molotov and were able to agree to supply all the materials asked for. This was only achieved, however, by Britain agreeing that certain materials and weapons supplied to her by America under the Lease-Lend Act, should be diverted to Russia, but the need was urgent, and drastic measures had to be adopted to ensure that it was met in time.

The third great German offensive opened on 1 October. It consisted of three thrusts towards Moscow, via Kalinin, in the north, via Vyazma and Mojaisk, in the centre, and via Orel, Bryansk and Kaluga in the south. Into this great offensive the Germans threw the whole weight of their mechanized divisions, heavily supported by aircraft and motorized infantry. By the 7th, the Russians had been forced to evacuate Orel, and five days later, after the most stubborn fighting, the Germans captured Bryansk. This was followed by the capture of Vyazma on the 13th and by the 14th the Germans had reached Mojaisk, only sixty-five miles south-west of the capital. On the 19th, after the fall of Kalinin and Kaluga, it looked as if the fall of Moscow was imminent.

STATE OF SIEGE IN MOSCOW

On this day the Russians announced that the Germans had massed four panzer armies, consisting of about 4,500 tanks each along the front between Kalinin and Orel in a final effort to break through by sheer weight of numbers. In view of this threat an Order of the Day was issued by Stalin declaring that Moscow would be defended to the last. At the same time a state of siege was proclaimed in the capital, where thousands of men, women and children laboured day and night to construct anti-tank defences, pill-boxes and fortifications of all kinds. The Government, too, was temporarily removed to Kuibyshev, on the middle Volga.

FINNISH ARTILLERY IN ACTION. The Finns declared war on Russia on 25 June, 1941, and launched attacks on Soviet territory near Murmansk, Lakes Onega and Ladoga, and in the Karelian Isthmus, the last being a direct threat to Leningrad. Although supported by German troops and aircraft, the Finns were able to make little progress against the strong Russian forces which they encountered. Above: Finnish guns on railway mountings are seen in action on the Karelian sector during the German-Finnish attacks on Leningrad.

But reinforcements were coming to the aid of the beleaguered capital. Large numbers of fresh Siberian and Mongolian troops arrived to swell the ranks of Marshal Timoshenko's army, and tanks and fighter planes from Britain and America were beginning to arrive in increasing numbers. The German advance was slowed down by violent Russian counter-attacks, and the seriousness of the German losses was shown by the fact that they were forced to withdraw troops from the Leningrad front and employ increasing numbers of Rumanian, Finnish, Hungarian and Italian troops in their assault.

Nevertheless, the German pressure was kept up and on 30 October mention was made in a Russian communique of fighting near Tula. This threatened the capital from the south. By the end of the month, however, the Russians were still fighting well and holding the enemy at all points. In addition weather conditions were rapidly deteriorating and snow, rain and mud were beginning to influence the course of the operations.

While the main battle for Moscow was in full swing, the German armies were keeping up stiff pressure farther south where they were making steady advances towards the industrial area of the Donets, north of the Sea of Azov, and towards the important town of Rostov-on-Don, key to the Caucasus. On 6 October Berdiansk, on the Sea of Azov, fell into their hands, and a week later the enemy were in Mariupol and advancing towards their next objective, Taganrog, which fell on the 18th.

This advance was responsible for the Russian evacuation of the Black Sea port of Odessa which, for the past two months, had been holding out stubbornly against the most violent attacks by Rumanian and German troops. The evacuation was carried out in perfect order over a period of eight days after the defenders had destroyed all important works and buildings of value to the enemy.

ADVANCE IN THE CRIMEA

Farther north the fall of Stalino on 20 October and of Kharkov on the 25th, robbed the Russians of two important industrial towns, but again the victories were hollow ones, for the Russians had removed most of their valuable plant, raw materials and stores, and blown up what they could not take.

Throughout October the Germans made repeated attempts to force their way through to the narrow Perekop Isthmus into the Crimea, but the Russian defences, ably supported by the guns of the Black Sea fleet, held firm and it was not until the last few days of the month that the Germans, after flinging seven divisions supported by two hundred aircraft into the battle, finally effected a break through and began to advance towards Simferopol and Feodosia.

FIFTH MOSCOW OFFENSIVE

November opened with the Germans forcing the pace on all fronts, but there were distinct signs of a stiffening of Russian resistance. On the 3rd the fifth German offensive against Moscow was launched, but the defenders counter-attacked strongly and held the enemy at all points. In the Tula area strong attacks by General Guderian's panzer units were repulsed with heavy losses, and the Russians even succeeded in advancing several miles. At Volokolamsk, too, local gains were made. The growing strength of the Russian resistance was admitted in Berlin where it was stated that the Russians were constantly bringing up fresh reserves and were employing all kinds of weapons, including rocket bombs which were used by Stormovik dive bombers for attacking tanks.

The failure of this offensive to gain any real ground was a serious blow to the enemy. The German troops were not properly equipped for winter warfare and it was therefore essential that Moscow should be taken and winter quarters thereby provided for the invading armies.

On 14 November, therefore, Hitler gave orders that the capital was to be taken at all costs, and two days later in compliance with his orders, a new offensive was launched into which the enemy threw a million men and some ten thousand tanks in a last tremendous effort to force a decision.

But still the Russians fought back. Supported by British-made tanks and fresh reserves they contested every inch of ground, their elastic lines bending under the strain, but never breaking. Serious situations developed at Tula, Stalinogorsk in the south, and Klin and Volokolamsk in the north, but although the enemy made advances at these points, their losses were so great that even the mighty German Army could not stand the strain.

This great battle continued throughout November, and in the early days of December the Germans made their final bid to reach Moscow. Having failed to encircle the capital, they made a colossal frontal attack in the direction of Mojaisk, which fell on 6 December. The Russian

RUSSIANS DESTROY DNIEPER DAM. After their evacuation of Dnepropetrovsk on 28 August, the Russians destroyed the huge dam at Zaporozhe to prevent it and its valuable machinery falling into enemy hands. The dam, one of the largest of its kind in the world, was built under the first Five Year Plan: it was capable of generating nearly 1,000,000 horse power, and its destruction had the effect of paralysing all the important industrial undertakings in the Eastern Ukraine. Above: the charges that reduced it to a heap of rubble are seen exploding.

13

German advance in Russia August—December, 1941

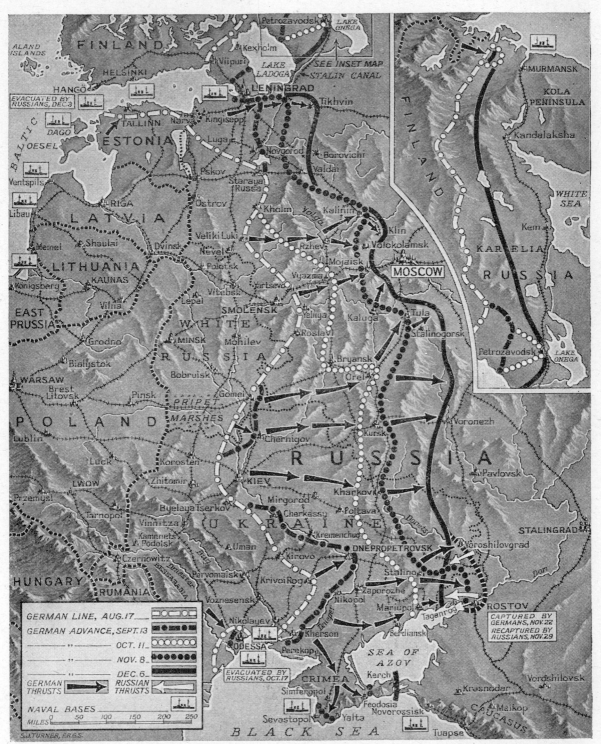

THE CAMPAIGN IN RUSSIA. Map showing stages of the German advances on the Eastern Front from 17 August to 6 December, when the offensive was brought to a standstill. During this period the most serious threats to Leningrad, Moscow and the Caucasus developed and the Russians were forced to evacuate some of their most valuable industrial towns. Losses on both sides, both in men and material, were tremendous, but the Russians succeeded in holding on and forced the enemy to embark upon a dreaded winter campaign.

counter-attacks north and south of the capital, were forcing the enemy on to the defensive, with the result that no advance could be made in the centre without running the risk of encirclement.

The fall of Mojaisk marked the turning point of the assault on Moscow. It was the final German attempt to gain winter quarters before the full force of the Russian winter came to the aid of the gallant defenders of freedom in the East. The attempt failed. From now on the initiative was to pass into Russian hands and the invincible armies of the Reich were to experience for the first time the bitterness of fighting on the defensive.

The losses in manpower and material during the fighting for Moscow were tremendous on both sides. Between 16 November and 10 December alone the Germans were reported to have lost 85,000 men killed, 1,434 tanks, 3,416 lorries, 675 guns, 339 mortars and 870 machine guns, besides vast numbers of aeroplanes.

On the other fronts during November and December the Germans were throwing masses of men into the battle. The fiercest fighting during this period was in the Crimea where, after gaining a foothold in late October, they captured Simferopol. This was rapidly followed by a move which split the Russian armies and forced them to fall back in two halves, one towards the naval base of Sevastopol and the other one towards Kerch. Feodosia fell on 3 November and Yalta on the 8th, and when on the 16th the Russians had to abandon Kerch, and carry out an evacuation of the peninsula across the narrow straits, things looked very black.

ROSTOV LOST AND REGAINED

In the Ukraine the German attempts to capture Rostov and to gain control of the Donets continued unabated in face of the most determined resistance. By 21 November the enemy had penetrated the suburbs of Rostov and on the following day, after bitter street fighting, the Russians were forced to withdraw to new lines farther east. This success, however, was short-lived, for in the early hours of 28 November the Russians attacked across the Don south-east of the town and penetrated the city. The following night another attack from the north-west was carried out with the result that the German forces in the city were practically encircled. After bitter fighting the remnants of von Kleist's forces broke and retreated towards Taganrog.

Farther north, in the Donets, the German advance continued to make slow progress from Kursk and Kharkov towards the towns of Voronezh and Pavlovsk, but when the main thrusts at Moscow and Rostov failed fighting died down in this region and the initiative slowly but surely passed into Russian hands.

All this time Leningrad, though encircled, repelled all German attacks. The most notable events during this period were the fall of Tikhvin, 100 miles east of the city, on 9 November, and the evacuation of Hango by the Russians on 3 December.

Little has been said about the attacks in the far north, where Murmansk was the main objective. Here the Finns launched various attacks in an effort to cut the railway carrying supplies from that port to the interior, but although communications were at times interfered with, no real advances were made.

HITLER'S EXCUSE

The failure of the German armies to reach their objectives was attributed by Hitler "not to the enemy, but to forty degrees of frost"; nevertheless, he showed his disapproval by dismissing von Bock, commander on the central front, and replacing him by Field Marshal List. The retreats which followed were explained to the German people as tactical withdrawals dictated by the fact that Germany no longer had any strategic ambitions for the winter.

Mr. Churchill in his review of the war on 11 December gave other reasons. "Six weeks or a month ago," he said, "people were wondering how soon Moscow would be taken, or Leningrad, in the north, or how soon the Germans would overrun the Caucasus and seize the oilfields of Baku. . . . Since then a striking change has become evident. The enormous power of the Russian armies and the glorious steadfastness and energy with which they have resisted the frightful onslaught made upon them have now been made plain.

"On top of this has come the Russian winter, and on top of that the Russian Air Force. Hitler forced his armies into this barren and devastated land. He has everywhere been brought to a standstill. On a large portion of the front he is in retreat; the sufferings of his troops are indescribable. . . . In Hitler's launching of this Nazi campaign on Russia we can already see after less than six months of fighting, that he made one of the outstanding blunders of history, and the results so far realized constitute an event of cardinal importance in the final decision of the war."

LENINGRAD IN DANGER. After capturing Novgorod on 27 August and the Estonian town of Tallinn on 2 September, the German forces attacking Leningrad pressed on to Luga, which they reached on the 3rd. Here violent Russian counter-attacks momentarily stayed their advance. In accordance with an order from Hitler to take the city at all costs, however, General von Leeb threw masses of fresh men and material into the battle, regardless of huge losses, and on 7 September the German High Command announced that mobile divisions with strong air support had reached the River Neva on a broad front and had captured Schlüsselburg, twenty-five

miles east of the city.   This, together with the Finnish thrusts on the Karelian Isthmus and between Lakes Ladoga and Onega completely cut off Leningrad from outside communication.   Meanwhile, in the city itself the whole population was mobilized ready if necessary to defend their homes to the last.   The photographs show: left, a Russian armoured train, its A.A. guns ready for instant action, on its way to the front line; top, right, German infantry entering a blazing village, set on fire by the Russians before withdrawing; bottom, right, Russian peasants who have been forced to leave their homes in a town that has just been occupied by the Germans.

17

GERMANS HANG RUSSIAN CIVILIANS. The many reports of German brutality in the occupied towns and villages in Russia are strikingly confirmed by this remarkable series of photographs found on a dead German officer. They illustrate the callous hanging of five Russian civilians near the town of Velizh, in the

Smolensk region, in September, and show: (1) The victims being paraded before an officer who is sentencing them to death; (2) Climbing on to the platform of the gibbet for a soldier to fix the nooses round their necks; (3) Nazi soldiers about to remove the platform; (4) The dead bodies of the five victims after the hanging.

BRITAIN'S GROWING AIR OFFENSIVE. On 7 September, the first anniversary of the first German mass attack on London, a strong bomber force, which included Britain's latest four-engined "Stirlings" and "Halifaxes," gave Berlin its heaviest bombing of the war so far. The raid, which was carried out in bright moonlight, lasted for two hours and extensive damage was caused to buildings, factories, warehouses and railway yards. The

weight of the attack was shown by the German Press, which called the raid "one of the most rotten and disgusting ever made on Berlin." The Berlin raid, together with raids on Kiel and Boulogne cost the R.A.F. twenty bombers. The pictures show: left, a "Stirling" crew watching their aircraft being bombed up ready for the night's operations; top, right, a "Halifax" heavy bomber in flight; below, a formation of Stirlings.

21

SPITSBERGEN COAL MINES DESTROYED. On 8 September the War Office told the story of a landing on Spitsbergen by a mixed force of British, Canadian and Norwegian troops under Canadian command. Its object was to prevent the enemy using the island's coal supplies, since it had become known that they had planned to seize all the coal for purposes of war transport. The operation was carried out unopposed; all the mines were completely destroyed, and all the inhabitants—some 700 miners and their families—were brought back to Britain where men of military age enlisted with the Royal Norwegian forces. Spitsbergen, which

lies 240 miles north of Norway within the Arctic circle, had been completely cut off from its parent state ever since the German occupation of Norway in April, 1940, and although not actually occupied by the enemy, German mining experts were known to have paid several visits to the island in order to examine its potentialities. The pictures show: top, left, plant and machinery at a mining power station put out of action by British sappers; bottom, left, miners and their families, with their luggage and personal belongings, about to embark in the landing barges; right, fuel dumps blazing as the Allied force prepared to re-embark.

U-BOAT SURRENDERS TO COASTAL COMMAND. On 8 September, the Admiralty announced that a German U-boat had been attacked in the Atlantic by a "Hudson" aircraft and forced to surrender. After wirelessing for naval and air relief, the "Hudson" guarded her prey for three and a half hours until a "Catalina" flying boat arrived to take over. After a further seven hours naval vessels arrived and took the U-boat into port. The picture shows a British officer in a Carley float approaching the U-boat to receive its surrender.

TANK BATTLES IN THE UKRAINE. Whilst the battle for Leningrad continued unabated, the Russian armies farther south counter-attacked fiercely in the Smolensk and Gomel areas thereby seriously threatening the German flanks. In order to relieve this pressure the enemy began a new attack on Kiev which resulted in the fall of Chernigov, to the north of the city, on the 12th and of Kremenchug, on the Dnieper, on the 14th. The German tanks seen above are advancing through heavy Russian artillery fire towards objectives in the Ukraine.

GERMAN TANKS GO FORWARD. During the fighting in the Ukraine, where the vast plains offered ideal country for tank warfare, the Germans threw masses of armoured vehicles into the battle. Against these the

Russians employed dive bombers and artillery, as well as their own armoured forces. The picture of a tank battle in progress shows German tanks advancing through an artillery barrage from Russian batteries.

SEPTEMBER, 1941. German infantry are here seen passing at the double through a blazing Russian village which has been "scorched" by its inhabitants. Scenes such as this were common on all parts of the Russian front during the German advance.

"HURRICANES" ON THE EASTERN FRONT. It was announced on 14 September that a fighter wing of the R.A.F. had arrived on the Russian front where it was co-operating with the Red Air Force. The wing, which was composed of "Hurricanes," was commanded by Wing Commander G. R. Isherwood, who had with him some of Britain's most experienced fighter pilots. The pictures show: above, some of the members of the wing watching one of their aircraft about to land; below, pilots inside a dispersal hut awaiting a call to action.

GERMANS ENTER UKRAINIAN CAPITAL. After crossing the Dnieper at Kremenchug the forces of von Runstedt switched northwards and linked up with those of von Bock advancing southwards from Chernigov. This manœuvre completely encircled the capital together with large bodies of Russian troops. As a result the evacuation of Kiev was carried out on 19 September, leaving the Russian armies to fight their way out of the German ring. Above, two German soldiers are seen looking out across the captured city from the citadel.

GERMANS IN BURNING KIEV. Before the Russians evacuated Kiev they carried out a systematic and thorough demolition of all plants and buildings likely to be of use to the enemy, so that when the Germans entered the city all that greeted them was a blazing inferno. The pictures show: top, a party of German shock troops assaulting a Russian position on the outskirts of the city prior to their entry into the town; below, buildings in the centre of Kiev left blazing by the retreating Russians; right, German soldiers in one of the city's main thoroughfares watching a blazing building, the walls of which have just collapsed into the road.

WAR FLAMES IN KIEV. Another dramatic picture of the Ukrainian capital as the Russians left it is shown above. The sacrifices made by the Russians in carrying out the "scorched earth" policy were a striking tribute to their determination to defeat the enemy at all costs by denying him much of the fruits of his victories.

BRITISH DEPORT NAZIS IN IRAN. After the Anglo-Russian occupation of Iran in August, the Iranian Government agreed to close all enemy legations and to hand over enemy nationals for internment. There was considerable delay, however, in carrying out these demands, and, as a result of strong protests by Britain and Russia, the Shah abdicated on 16 September and was succeeded by his son. As many enemy nationals were still hiding in the country, British and Russian troops advanced to the outskirts of Teheran on the 17th, and on the 18th Soviet parachute troops occupied the airfields and barracks in the vicinity. The next day all the remaining Germans who had been sheltering in the legation were deported. The pictures show: above, British armoured cars en route to the capital; below, the luggage of the Germans being removed from the capital in lorries.

Baltic Islands in German hands

GERMANS CAPTURE RUSSIAN AIR BASE. On 20 September German storm troops were landed from barges on the Estonian islands of Worms, Moon and Œsel, which lie at the mouth of the Gulf of Riga. Of these Œsel was the most important, for it was from here that Russian bombers carried out raids on Germany. Landings were first carried out on Worms and Moon, and later German troops fought their way across the dam between Moon and Œsel and succeeded in gaining a foothold. Fresh troops and supplies, landed from transports, soon enabled the enemy to advance, and before the day was out Arensburg, the chief town and seaport of the island, was in their hands. The pictures show: above, German troops and equipment being landed on Moon; right, Nazi troops repairing the dam between Moon and Œsel which had been dynamited by the Russians with the object of holding up the German advance.

BRITISH SUCCESS IN ABYSSINIA. After the fall of Amba Alagi, in May, the only remaining Italian resistance in the country was centred round Gondar. On 28 September, however, British and patriot forces attacked and captured the Italian garrison of Wolshefit, an important position guarding Gondar from the north. The Italian commander, Colonel Gonella, his staff, and 3,000 troops were taken prisoner, and the way was paved for an assault upon Gondar itself. The pictures show : above, Colonel Gonella with his surrendering force passing the guard of honour of King's African Rifles; below, some of the Italian colonial troops who took part in the battle.

BRITAIN AND U.S.A. AGREE TO HELP RUSSIA. On 29 September, the Three Power Supply Conference between Britain, U.S.A. and Russia opened in Moscow under the chairmanship of M. Molotov in order to examine all the available resources of the Soviet Government in conjunction with the production capacity of Britain and the U.S. The conference was carried out by six committees—on Navy, Army, Aviation, Raw Materials, Transportation and Medical Supplies—who studied the Russian requirements and decided whether or not they could be met. On 30 September, Lord Beaverbrook and Mr. Averell Harriman, the heads of the British and U.S. missions, visited Stalin in the Kremlin to give their final replies to the Russian requests. This interview is best described in Lord Beaverbrook's own words: "The interpreter (M. Litvinov) began solemnly

and anxiously to read out each item. Most things we were ready to supply, and the answers came straight from Harriman or me. He said 'agreed' if the item concerned the U.S. I said 'okay' when Britain was producing the supplies. As the list rolled on Litvinov sprang up from his seat crying out with enthusiasm. Stalin's relief was manifest. He was satisfied." Britain and the U.S. between them were able to agree to all the requests of the Soviet Government, and it was not long before the results of this conference were seen in tanks, aeroplanes and other munitions of war which were being transported in vast quantities to the Russian front. The pictures show: top, Lord Beaverbrook and M. Molotov signing the agreement; left, Lord Beaverbrook arriving by air in Moscow; right, with Mr. Averell Harriman (hand on hat) on his return to London.

H.M.S. "NELSON" HIT BY TORPEDO. On 30 September, the Admiralty announced that an important British convoy had been recently attacked by Italian aircraft in the Mediterranean. Escorting naval forces accounted for thirteen enemy planes by putting up a terrific barrage from which only one attacker escaped. During a second attack the battleship "Nelson" was hit by a torpedo, but only slightly damaged. The attacker was shot down by naval fighters. The photograph shows the enemy machine actually attacking; the splash on the right is the torpedo hitting the water. The bursts of shells from "Nelson's" A.A. guns are clearly visible.

Negotiations for exchange of prisoners fail

HOSPITAL SHIPS AT NEWHAVEN. On 6 October, negotiations for the exchange of seriously wounded prisoners of war broke down after a first batch of Germans had been embarked. The ships should have left on the 4th for Dieppe where they would have taken on board British prisoners for the return journey. Negotiations, which were conducted by direct wireless, failed because Germany, at the last moment, insisted upon the exchange being made on a purely numerical basis. Above, the hospital ships, brilliantly illuminated, are seen at Newhaven waiting to leave; below, men of the R.A.M.C. are carrying out a disembarkation rehearsal.

THE BATTLE FOR LENINGRAD. Throughout September the battle for Leningrad continued with undiminished violence, but despite the fact that the Germans, in accordance with Hitler's orders to take the city at all costs, threw masses of men into the line regardless of loss, they were unable to break through the strong Russian

defences. Early in October, Russian counter-attacks south, east and west of the city forced the attackers on to the defensive, whilst in the Karelian Isthmus, where the Finns were threatening the city, severe casualties were inflicted on the enemy. Above, a town on the Karelian Isthmus is seen after an attack by Russian bombers.

RUSSIANS LOSE MARIUPOL AND BERDIANSK. The German crossing of the Dnieper at Kremenchug was a serious threat to the Russian armies in the Ukraine. Not only did it help to bring about the fall of Kiev, but it threatened the whole of the Russian defences on the east bank of the Dnieper and made it imperative that they should straighten, and consequently shorten, their line. In addition, the enemy succeeded in ferrying troops across the wide lower reaches of the river under strong aerial protection, and in pushing on towards the Crimea. On 23 September fierce fighting was reported at Kherson, and a few days later the enemy had reached

the Perekop Isthmus and was endeavouring to force his way into the Crimea. Meanwhile another thrust along the shores of the Sea of Azov pushed the Russians back to Berdiansk and Mariupol, which fell on 6 and 14 October respectively. Farther north, where the great industrial city of Kharkov was threatened, the Russians launched counter-attacks, particularly in the Kursk area, with the object of relieving the enemy pressure. The pictures show: left, German infantry, supported by tanks, in action in the streets of Mariupol; right, the destruction of the railway station which was dynamited by Russian sappers just before they were obliged to evacuate the town.

RUSSIAN CAPITAL HOLDS OUT. The third German drive towards Moscow began on 1 October with pincer thrusts in the Roslavl and Kholm areas. By the 7th the enemy were in Orel and were exerting heavy pressure near Bryansk and Vyazma which resulted in the fall of these towns on the 12th and 13th respectively. Two days later a German column penetrated as far as Mojaisk, but was driven back by well-timed counter-attacks. The seriousness of the situation was admitted by the Russians who announced that the Germans were using about

18,000 tanks on this front alone. On the 19th, after the fall of Kalinin and Kaluga, Stalin issued an Order of the Day declaring that Moscow would be defended to the last man, and at the same time a state of siege was proclaimed in the capital. The pictures show: top, left, Russian prisoners captured during the fighting at Bryansk; bottom, left, men of the Hitler Corps passing through a burnt-out village; top, right, women and children sheltering from German artillery fire; bottom, right, a German tank passing through Vyazma on the Moscow road.

FRENCH PORT BOMBED. During October the R.A.F. carried out almost daily attacks on objectives in enemy-occupied France. Huge four-engined "Stirlings," like that seen above dodging enemy flak, took part in many of these raids as did also "Hurricane" fighters equipped to carry two 250-lb. bombs. The lower picture shows an attack by "Blenheims" on the docks at Havre on the 15th. The numbers indicate : (1) bombs bursting on a 12,000-ton tanker moored alongside the quay; (2) a direct hit with a heavy calibre bomb on a 5,000-ton merchant ship; (3) a near miss on a 9,500-ton vessel; (4) bombs bursting on the quay; (5) damage done to the roof o. a warehouse.

RUSSIANS EVACUATE ODESSA. The Black Sea port of Odessa was occupied by German and Rumanian forces on 16 October after a siege that had lasted since August. The evacuation, which was carried out in perfect order, was dictated by events in the Eastern Ukraine and the consequent need of more men to reinforce the Crimea where the enemy, after crossing the Dnieper, were trying to force an entry through the narrow Perekop Isthmus. Before leaving the port the Russians destroyed all important works. The pictures show: top, citizens cheering the Russian rearguard as they move up to the front line; below, German Panzer vehicles moving to the attack.

RUSSIANS LOSE TWO MORE TOWNS. After the fall of Mariupol on 14 October, the German forces in the Ukraine, assisted by Slovak and Hungarian divisions, continued their advance, and on the 20th captured the important armaments centre of Stalino. Farther south, mechanized divisions pushing along the coast of the Sea of Azov, made progress towards the important port and communications centre of Rostov-on-Don, beyond which

lay the valuable Caucasus oilfields. On the 22nd they captured Taganrog, between Mariupol and Rostov, after many days' fierce fighting which cost them 35,000 casualties, as well as large numbers of armoured vehicles, stores, and military equipment. The picture shows German troops entering Stalino; the chimneys in the background are those of an important steel factory that has been rendered useless by the retreating Russians.

FALL OF KHARKOV

25 TO 29 OCTOBER, 1941

Whilst the German armies in Southern Ukraine were hammering their way towards Rostov-on-Don, their armies farther north were exerting all their strength to reach the great industrial town of Kharkov. The defending forces, however, by repeated counter-attacks, managed to slow down enemy progress, but were unable to bring his advance to a standstill. By the 25th enemy advanced units had entered the suburbs of the city, where fierce hand-to-hand fighting took place in the streets, which were reported to be littered with German dead. On one day alone enemy casualties amounted to 3,500 dead, but in spite of these huge losses the Germans continued to throw fresh troops into the battle and on the 29th the Russians had to abandon the city. Before the evacuation, however, all the most important factories and plants, railway rolling stock and military stores were removed and other plants that could not be got away in time were blown up. The loss of this great town was a severe blow to the Russian cause for not only was it of first importance as a manufacturing centre, but it was a vital railway junction and supply centre for the Russian armies covering the Donets Basin. The German victory, however, was only achieved by great loss in men and material. According to Russian sources they lost nearly 120,000 men in killed and wounded as well as 450 tanks and armoured cars, nearly 3,000 lorries and more than 200 guns. The picture shows German troops, with tank support, fighting in the streets just before the town was abandoned by the Russian forces.

ASSAULT ON THE CRIMEA. Although the German offensive against the Crimea began on 27 September, it was not until 28 October that the enemy, by employing seven divisions, supported by large numbers of tanks, artillery and aircraft, succeeded in penetrating the Russian defences on the Perekop Isthmus and gaining a foothold on the peninsula. Here they succeeded in dividing the defending armies into two groups, one of which

retired towards the great naval base of Sevastopol and the other towards Kerch. On 1 November, Simferopol, only thirty miles from Sevastopol, fell, and two days later Feodosia, near the Kerch Strait, was in enemy hands. The pictures show: left, German infantry in the Perekop Isthmus leaving a trench to launch an attack on the Russian positions; right, German transport vehicles passing through Simferopol after the fall of the town.

LAST MOMENTS OF H.M.S. "ARK ROYAL." On 14 November, the Admiralty announced that the 23,000 ton aircraft carrier H.M.S. "Ark Royal" had been sunk in the Mediterranean by a torpedo from an enemy U-boat. Efforts were made to tow the ship into port, but she developed a heavy list and foundered before she reached her destination. Out of a complement of about 1,600 only one man lost his life. The picture shows a British destroyer taking off the crew of the doomed ship shortly before she foundered. H.M.S. "Ark Royal," most famous of all

British aircraft carriers, was the third ship of this type to be lost since war began. During her career on active service she had steamed some 205,000 miles and engaged in thirty-two war operations. She served in the Norwegian campaign, participated in the hunt for the "Graf Spee," and her aircraft torpedoed the German battleship "Bismarck" on 26 May. She served in the North and South Atlantic before joining Admiral Somerville's force in the Mediterranean. Both the Germans and the Italians claimed to have sunk her on several occasions.

NEUTRALITY ACT REVISED. In view of the frequency of Axis attacks on U.S. ships, the Senate on 13 November recommended the amendment of Sections 2, 3 and 6 of the Neutrality Act, and on the same day the House of Representatives gave its approval by 212 votes to 194. The President signed the Bill revising the Act on the

18th, and on the same day the Navy Department announced that 300 to 400 ships would be armed immediately, first preference being given to those serving Britain and Northern Europe, and second to those operating to and from the Red Sea. Above: men are seen at work on a gun that is being fitted to a U.S. merchant ship.

SECOND BRITISH OFFENSIVE IN LIBYA

18 NOVEMBER, 1941

At dawn on 18 November, Imperial forces under the command of Lieut.-General Sir Alan Cunningham, with strong air support, crossed the Egyptian frontier into Cyrenaica on a broad front from the coast east of Sollum to as far south as Jarabub. The object of this attack was to engage and destroy German and Italian forces who were massing on the frontier and constituting a threat to Egypt, and to regain if possible the territory which had been lost during General Rommel's advance of the previous spring. For some months before the attack was launched the British forces had been steadily reinforced with men, tanks and aircraft, many of the tanks being of American manufacture. These forces had been skilfully dispersed, and camouflage had been used to such good effect that when the advance began very little opposition was encountered either from the air or from ground forces. Pressure was rapidly exerted on Axis forces holding positions from Helafaya to Sidi Omar where British armoured formations, with New Zealand, South African and Indian troops in support crossed the frontier and penetrated some fifty miles into enemy territory. The R.A.F., and the Australian and South African Air Forces, gave strong support to the troops on the ground, and during the day destroyed between them eighteen Axis aircraft besides bombing enemy transport on the Benina road, near Benghazi. The picture shows a line of British tanks moving out to attack the enemy.

BRITISH CAPTURE
In the evening of 19 November British advance forces captured Sidi Rezegh, southeast of Tobruk, and on the following day battle was joined with strong German armoured forces. After losing seventy tanks, thirty-three armoured cars and several hundred prisoners the Germans withdrew. On the 21st a heavy tank battle began in the Sidi Rezegh-Gabr Saleh-Capuzzo triangle, but Gen. Cunningham was able to interpose his forces between the main German

SIDI REZEGH

tank strength to the east and a smaller force to the west. The enemy made three attempts to break through, but was driven back with heavy losses. The pictures show: top, enemy tanks ablaze after being blown up by South African troops; left, a knocked-ou German tank and a captured armoured car; left, below, a British column moving across an enemy minefield; right, captured German guns; right, below, troops negotiating barbed wire.

GERMAN TANKS BREAK OUT. The tank battle around Sidi Rezegh continued until 28 November, when there was a pause. During this time General Rommel had been trying, without success, to break through the British ring and effect a junction with his troops to the west. Sidi Rezegh itself changed hands several times. Meanwhile New Zealand infantry pushing westwards along the coast occupied Bardia on the 22nd and Gambut on the 23rd, and on the 27th succeeded in linking up at El Duda with a force that had sallied out from Tobruk. During the next few days these troops gradually widened their corridor of contact, but on the 29th the Sidi Rezegh battle

flared up once more. After several unsuccessful attempts to break through to the west, Rommel concentrated all his available tanks on a narrow front and on 1 December succeeded in hammering his way through the Tobruk corridor by sheer weight of armour. The R.A.F. and R.A.A.F. played a prominent part in these operations, bombing enemy communications and harassing his ground forces with machine gun and cannon fire. The fighter pilots in the above picture are members of an Australian Army Co-operation Squadron equipped with American-built "Tomahawk" fighters. They are running to their aircraft in answer to an urgent order to attack the enemy.

CONQUEST OF
ABYSSINIA COMPLETE

27 NOVEMBER, 1941

Just before dawn on 27 November an intense artillery bombardment was opened up on Gondar, last remaining centre of Italian resistance in Abyssinia, and the town was heavily bombed from the air. This was followed soon after daybreak by a general assault from several directions by British, Empire and Allied Forces under the command of Major General C. C. Fowkes. After capturing the advanced enemy positions at Deffeccia and Maldiba, Gondar itself was stormed by East African troops who, by the evening, had gained complete control of the town. At 6 p.m. the Italian commander, General Nasi, surrendered with all his forces, amounting to about 10,000 men, half of whom were Italians. This victory brought the campaign in East Africa to a successfu conclusion. The pictures show: top, Italian prisoners marching through Gondar under escort; left, men of the King's African Rifles marching past the saluting base during a ceremonial parade held to celebrate the victorious finish of the war in Abyssinia.

ROSTOV LOS

After the fall of Taganro
on 22 October, the Russia
forces on the souther
front retreated slowl
towards Rostov-on-Do:
about forty miles farthe
east. This town owes i
importance to its navig
tional facilities and i
position on three key ra
ways. The Russians en
ployed skilful delayir
tactics and blew up th
Don dykes thereby inu
dating large tracts
country between the tov
and the Sea of Azov.
addition Soviet guerrill
were especially acti
behind the enemy line
Nevertheless, on 22 No
ember, just a month aft
the fall of Taganrog, t
Germans entered t
town. Their victory, how
ever, was short lived. C

AND REGAINED

the 28th, the Soviet 57th
Army, commanded by
General Remizov, re-
entered Rostov from the
south-west and on the following day the 9th Army
fought its way into the
town from the north-
east, thereby practically
encircling the Germans
who, after two days of
fierce street fighting in
which they lost more than
1,000 men killed, beat a
disorganized retreat. The
pictures show: top,
German troops passing
through Taganrog, where
factories and other buildings are blazing furiously;
left, Russian soldiers
hunting down German
stragglers in Rostov;
right, citizens welcom-
ing Russian troops when
they re-entered the town.

GERMANS AT THE GATES OF MOSCOW. The great German bid to take Moscow continued unabated through-out October and November, but the enemy made slow progress. Klin and Volokolamsk fell on 26 and 28 November respectively, but strong counter-attacks near Tula and Klin upset the German plans to encircle the capital. Early in December the enemy threw every available man and tank into a gigantic frontal attack ; Mojaisk fell on the 6th and advance units actually penetrated to within about thirty miles of the capital after some of the bloodiest fighting of the campaign. But they got no farther. Thereafter the initiative passed steadily into Russian hands as winter's icy grip descended upon the scene of battle. The pictures show: top, left, Moscow citizens digging anti-tank ditches at the approaches to the city ; below, left, Cossack cavalry attacking an enemy position near the city on foot ; above, ill-clad German soldiers, only one of whom is wearing a greatcoat, with horse transport, retreating north of Moscow ; below, a big Russian tank passing through the capital on its way to the front line only a few miles away.

BOMBING OF PEARL HARBOUR. The great U.S. naval base is here shown during the height of the Japanese attack. The explosion was caused by a direct hit on the magazine of the destroyer "Shaw"

JAPAN DECLARES WAR ON BRITAIN AND THE UNITED STATES

SUNDAY, 7 DECEMBER, 1941

At dawn on the morning of 8 December (7 December according to British time) a force of about 150 Japanese bombers and torpedo-carrying aircraft launched a surprise attack on Pearl Harbour, Hawaii, the chief U.S. naval base in the Pacific. Hits were scored on several naval craft lying at anchor in the harbour and two battleships, the "Oklahoma" and the "Arizona" were sunk. Other military objectives in the island, including Hickam airfield, were attacked and considerable damage was done. The casualties amounted to 3,000, 1,500 of which were fatal. Japanese aircraft also bombed Davao and Baguio, in the Philippine Islands, and dropped leaflets urging the Filipinos to rise against their "American oppressors." It was not until later in the day that the formal declaration of war against Britain and the U.S. was made. In China, Japanese troops occup.ed the International Settlement at Shanghai and the British and U.S. concessions at Tientsin.

Japan's entry into the war, although sudden, was not unexpected. Ever since the previous October when the direction of Japan's foreign policy had fallen into the hands of the military clique under the leadership of General Tojo, that country's relations with Britain and the U.S. had steadily worsened. The new premier had demanded a free hand to liquidate the "China incident" once and for all, and had declared that until Britain and America refrained from supplying arms to China and recognized Japan's leadership in the Western Pacific no peaceful settlement was likely to be reached. On 14 November, however, a special Japanese envoy, Mr. Saburo Kurusu, arrived in America to aid Admiral Nomura, Japanese Ambassador to Washington, in the latter's talks with the U.S. Government. Three days later General Tojo announced a three-point programme upon which, he said, the success of these negotiations depended. The points were: 1, Third powers must refrain from obstructing the successful conclusion of the China affair; 2, Countries surrounding Japan must refrain from presenting a military menace to the Empire, and must nullify such hostile measures as economic blockade; 3, Must exert their utmost efforts to prevent an extension of the European war to East Asia. On 6 December President Roosevelt sent a personal note to the Emperor of Japan, but before any reply was received, and whilst the Washington talks were still proceeding, the attack on Pearl Harbour announced that Japan had entered the war in true Axis fashion by striking first and declaring war afterwards.

7 DECEMBER, 1941. During the Japanese attack on Pearl Harbour the 32,600-ton U.S. battleship "Arizona" received a direct hit. Here she is seen ablaze shortly before she sank

ROOSEVELT SIGNS WAR DECLARATION. On 8 December Britain and the United States formally declared war on Japan. In the U.S., President Roosevelt addressed a joint session of Congress (above) after which a resolution was introduced in both Houses and adopted with one dissenting vote. The President signed the

declaration shortly afterwards at the White House. Three days later Germany and Italy declared war on the United States and on the same day President Roosevelt obtained the approval of both Houses to declarations of war against these countries. Never before had there been a greater challenge to liberty and civilization.

SIEGE OF SEVASTOPOL. After capturing Feodosia, the German forces in the Crimea drove eastwards and on 16 November captured the town of Kerch thereby compelling the Russian forces to carry out a hazardous withdrawal across the Kerch straits. Meanwhile, on the west of the Crimea, the enemy had thrown three armoured and nine infantry divisions against the defences of the great Russian naval base of Sevastopol, but the Russian line held firm and tremendous losses were inflicted upon the attackers. The picture shows grief-stricken Russian parents who have just found the body of their son who was killed in the fighting in the Crimea.

GERMAN REVERSE NEAR LENINGRAD. Although the Germans succeeded in encircling Leningrad, their efforts to take it by storm failed. Nevertheless, during October and November, they pushed slowly eastwards and on 29 November captured Tikhvin, 100 miles south-east of the city. On 8 December, however, Russian forces, under General Merezhkov, re-entered the town after a battle in which more than 7,000 Germans were killed and much valuable war material was captured intact. The pictures show: above, German horse transport retreating down a snow-covered road; below, Russian infantry following up their tanks during an attack on a village.

JAPANESE LAUNCH ATTACK ON MALAYA. On 8 December a fleet of Japanese transports, with stron
naval support, approached the mouth of the Kelantan River, North-east Malaya, and landings were carried out nort
of Kota Bahru. On the same day a British naval force which was steaming to intercept the enemy convoy
was heavily attacked with bombs and torpedoes by a strong force of Japanese bombers. H.M.S. "Princ

of Wales" and "Repulse" were hit several times and sunk. At the time of the attack the ships were without aerial protection owing to enemy attacks on the aerodromes from which their land-based aircraft operated. Casualties amounted to 595 officers and men, among whom was Admiral Phillips, C.-in-C. of the China Station. The picture, specially drawn by Frank H. Mason, P.R.I., shows the crippled British ships during the height of the attack.

CAVITE IN FLAMES. At daybreak on 10 December strong Japanese forces, with strong naval and aerial protection, attempted landings on the wes: coast of Luzon, in the Philippines, between Vigan and San Fernando, but were repulsed by American and Filipino troops, and three enemy transports were destroyed by U.S. Aircraft. Some parachutists who had been dropped near Vigan were rounded up. Later in the day, however, fresh Japanese troops, in considerable force, established themselves at Aparri, on the northern tip of the island, and

empted to push southwards, heavily engaged by the defenders. During the day Manila, the chief town of zon and capital of the Philippine Islands, was twice raided by waves of Japanese bombers; attacks were made the Nichols airfield and Fort William McKinley, and considerable damage was done at the naval base of Cavite, Manila Bay, eight miles south-west of the capital, where 200 bombs were dropped. Casualties amounted to rty people killed and 300 wounded. Above: the water front at Cavite is seen ablaze after one of the raids.

GERMANS RETREAT BEFORE MOSCOW. After bringing the German offensive to a standstill on 6 December the Russian armies defending Moscow launched strong counter-attacks all along the line. On the 15th, after week's fierce fighting, they recaptured Klin, and on the same day Kalinin itself was in their hands. In the cen of the line heavy pressure was exerted near Mojaisk, whilst to the south of the capital, strong thrusts forced t

emy back to Kaluga, which fell on the 30th after changing hands several times. The pictures show: top, ndoned German guns and vehicles left behind by the enemy during their retreat from Klin; left, well-clad ssian soldiers advancing through a village on the Moscow front which has recently been cleared of the enemy; ht, blazing buildings in Kalinin set on fire by the enemy just before they were forced to evacuate the town.

HALIFAX AIRCRAFT
OVER TARGET

GNEISENAU

SCHARNHORST

GERMAN BATTLESHIPS BOMBED. Ever since March, when the German battle cruisers "Scharnhor
and "Gneisenau" entered the harbour at Brest to refuel after a raiding expedition in the Atlantic, these sh
had been repeatedly attacked by the R.A.F., and several direct hits had been scored. In May they were joir
by the heavy cruiser "Prinz Eugen" which had managed to reach port after the action in which the "Bismar
was sunk. Attacks on these three valuable ships continued throughout the year, and the fact that they w

PRINZ EUGEN

unable to put to sea showed that they had suffered considerable damage.   On 18 December a particularly heavy daylight attack was made on these ships by "Stirling," "Halifax" and "Manchester" bombers, strongly escorted by "Spitfire" and "Hurricane" squadrons. A great weight of bombs was dropped and direc hits were scored on the dry docks in which the ships were berthed. Five British bombers and one fighter were lost against an enemy loss of eight fighters. Above, "Halifax" bombers are seen over the target during the raid.

FIVE-DAY ATTACK ON MEDITERRANEAN CONVOY. On 17 December a British convoy of more than thirty ships, strongly protected by warships, was attacked in the Mediterranean by U-boats and aircraft. In spite of the fact that the a tack lasted for five days, until the 21st, almost without a break, only two merchant ships, totalling 6,198 tons, were sunk. At least three U-boats, and many enemy aircraft, including two

cke-Wulfs, were destroyed by the escorting warships. British naval losses amounted to one old
stroyer and one auxiliary vessel of 5,537 tons. The pictures show: above, an enemy torpedo bomber,
h its starboard engine on fire, about to crash into the sea after having been hit by A.A. fire from the cruiser
the right; below, a near miss on a British cruiser; one of the supply ships is seen on the right.

GERMAN RETREAT IN LIBYA. After breaking out of the ring which British and Imperial forces h
thrown round them, the Germans in Libya retreated rapidly, pursued by mobile columns and harassed
bombers and low-flying fighters which inflicted severe damage to their closely-packed formations. On
December Derna and Mekili were entered without opposition, and by the following day advance British forc
were within about eighty miles of Benghazi and still advancing. Above, a heavily loaded Indian transport colu
is seen passing through Derna with supplies and equipment for the troops in the forward are

FIGHTING IN LUZON. After the failure of their initial attempt to gain control of the Philippines, the Japanese, on 22 December, landed a force of about 100,000 men, together with tanks, in the Lingayen Gulf area of Luzon. Landings were also made on Mindanao, the second largest island of the group, where fighting took place in the Davao area. On this day, too, the small garrison of 400 Marines at Wake Island, the U.S. naval base, 3,000 miles to the north-east, surrendered after an heroic defence lasting fourteen days. The pictures above show ruins of the town of San Pablo, near Manila, after a severe raid carried out by Japanese bombers on Christmas Day.

"When we compare the resources of the United States and the British Empire with those of Japan, when we remember those of China, which has so valiantly withstood invasion and tyranny, and when also we observe the Russian menace which hangs over Japan it becomes difficult to reconcile Japan's action with prudence and sanity. What kind of a people do they think we are? Is it possible that they do not realize we shall never cease to persevere against them until they have been taught a lesson which they and the world will never forget?

BRITISH PREMIER ADDRESSES CONGRESS. On 22 December Mr. Winston Churchill, accompanied by Navy, Army, Air Force and Production chiefs, arrived in Washington where he discussed with President Roosevelt matters relating to the Anglo-U.S. war effort. Meetings were also held between Service, Economic and Production experts of the two countries and far-reaching decisions were made relating to the joint conduct of the war. In a public statement regarding the conversations Mr. Roosevelt said that as a result of the meetings the position of the United States, and all the nations aligned with her,

Here we are together facing a group of mighty foes who seek our ruin; here we are together defending all that which to free men is dear. . . . Twice in a single generation the catastrophe of world war has fallen upon us; twice in our lifetime has the long arm of fate reached across the ocean to bring the United States into the forefront of the battle itself. . . . I avow my hope and faith, sure and inviolate, that in the days to come the British and American peoples will for their own safety and for the good of all, walk together in majesty, in justice, and in peace."

had been strengthened immeasurably. "We have," he declared, "advanced far along the road towards achievement of the ultimate objective—the crushing defeat of these forces that attacked and made war on us." On 26 December Mr. Churchill addressed a joint session of the U.S. Senate and House of Representatives, by whom he was given an enthusiastic ovation. Above, he is seen making his historic speech which demonstrated the strong bond of kinship between the two great English-speaking democracies. Studies of the Premier during his address, and extracts from his speech are given inset.

BOMB BURSTS

SHELL BURSTS FROM GUNS OF ATTACKING FIGHTERS

FALL OF BENGHAZI. After capturing Derna, the Eighth Army continued its pursuit of the re-treating enemy forces. The main German Army was in the Soluk area, south-east of Benghazi, whilst Italians were concentrated along the coast north-east of the town. On 21 December British forces captured Cirene and Apollonia and exerted strong pressure on the Italians covering Benghazi, and on the next day mobile columns reached the coastal plain on the Gulf of Sirte. On Christmas Eve Benghazi was entered by the Royal Dragoons after it had been evacuated by the enemy, and the nearby aerodrome of Barce was captured by Indian troops. On the same day a mixed mobile column occupied Benina aerodrome. With the fall of Benghazi the whole of Cyrenaica, except for the isolated enemy garrisons at Sollum, Hela-faya and Bardia came under British control. The pictures show: top, an Axis column under aerial bombardment; left, bombs falling on Barce aerodrome; right, sunken Axis ships in Benghazi harbour.

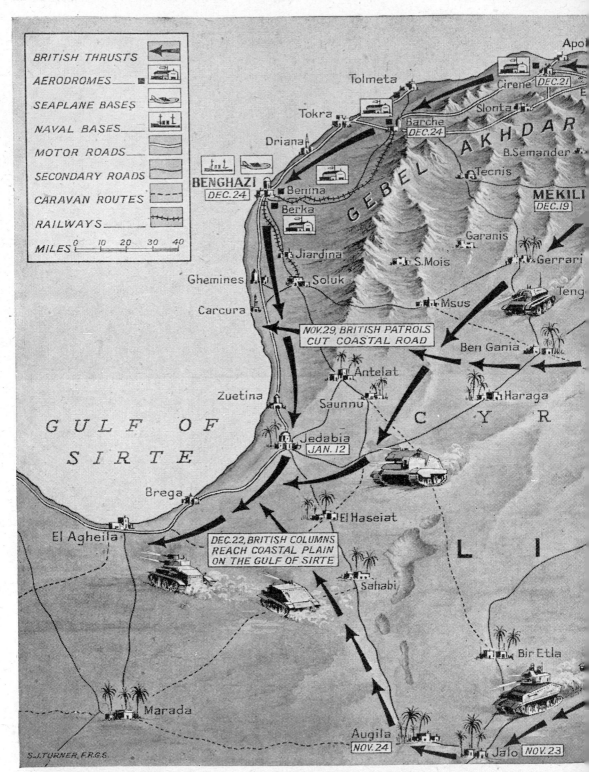

BRITISH THRUSTS
AERODROMES
SEAPLANE BASES
NAVAL BASES
MOTOR ROADS
SECONDARY ROADS
CARAVAN ROUTES
RAILWAYS
MILES   0   10   20   30   40

Apo

Tolmeta
Cirene   DEC.21
Slonta
Tokra   Barche   DEC.24
Driana   B.Semander
                         GEBEL AKHDAR
Tecnis
BENGHAZI   Benina   MEKILI
DEC.24   DEC.19
              Berka
                         Garanis
                         S.Mois   Gerrari
Jiardina
Ghemines   Soluk   Teng
Carcura   Msus
                  NOV.29, BRITISH PATROLS
                  CUT COASTAL ROAD   Ben Gania
                         Antelat
              Zuetina   Saunnu   Haraga
                                    C   Y   R
GULF OF
                         Jedabia
SIRTE   JAN.12
      Brega
                              El Haseiat
El Agheila   L   I
           DEC.22, BRITISH COLUMNS
           REACH COASTAL PLAIN
           ON THE GULF OF SIRTE
                              Sahabi
                                        Bir Etla
        Marada
S.J.TURNER, F.R.G.S.   Augila
                                    NOV.24
                                         Jalo   NOV.23

ADVANCE OF THE EIGHTH ARMY. Map showing the stages of the second British and Imperial advance
Libya from the opening of the offensive on 18 November until 17 January, on which date the Axis garrison
Helafaya surrendered. By this time the whole of Libya had been cleared of enemy forces except for a pocket

ffensive in Libya November, 1941—January, 1942

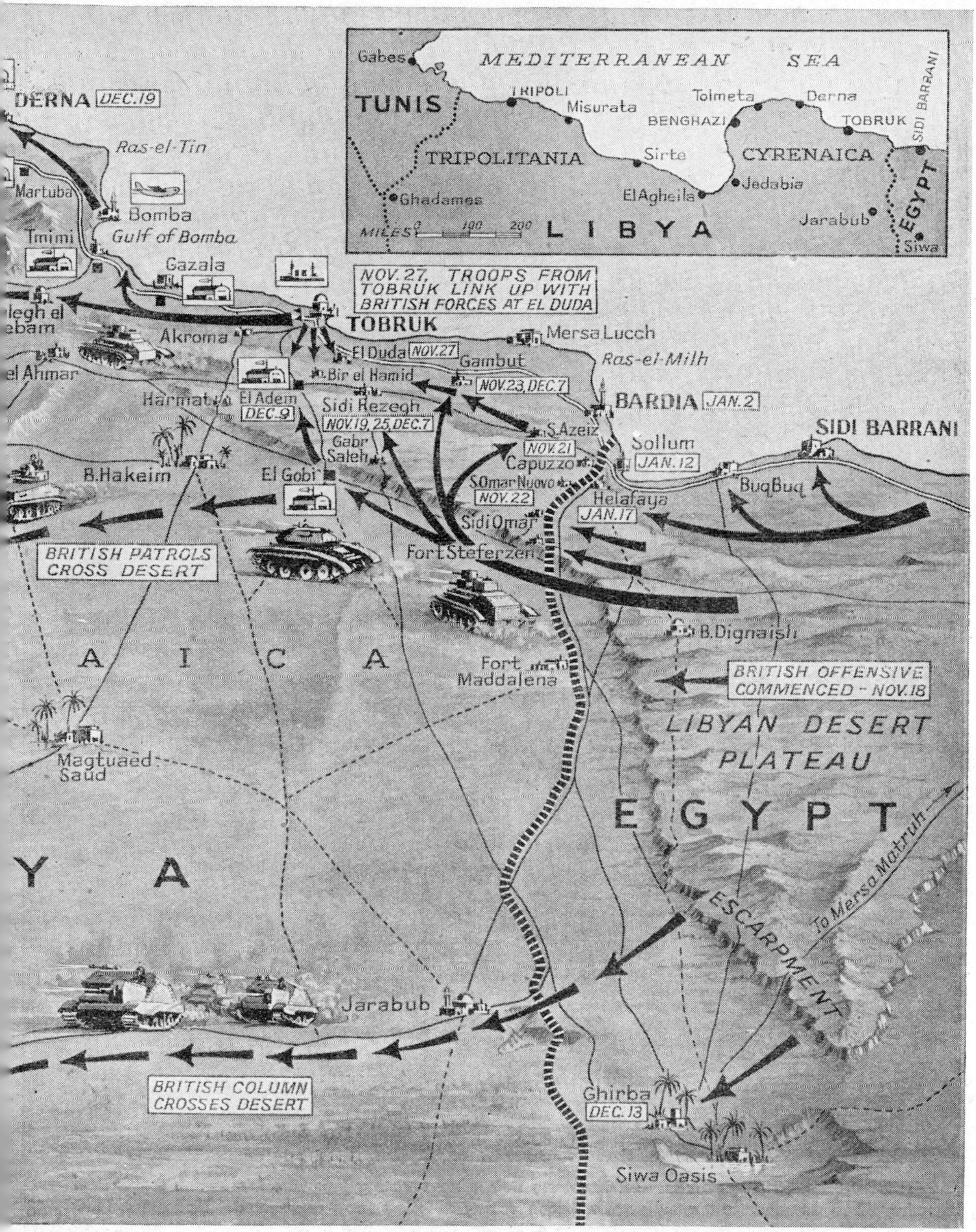
MEDITERRANEAN SEA
Gabes
TUNIS
TRIPOLI
Misurata
TRIPOLITANIA
Ghadames
Tolmeta
Derna
BENGHAZI
TOBRUK
SIDI BARRANI
Sirte
CYRENAICA
El Agheila
Jedabia
Jarabub
EGYPT
Siwa
MILES 0 100 200
LIBYA
DERNA DEC.19
Ras-el-Tin
Martuba
Bomba
Tmimi
Gulf of Bomba
Gazala
NOV.27, TROOPS FROM TOBRUK LINK UP WITH BRITISH FORCES AT EL DUDA
TOBRUK
Akroma
Mersa Lucch
El Duda NOV.27
Gambut
Ras-el-Milh
el Ahmar
Bir el Hamid
NOV.23, DEC.7
Harmat
El Adem DEC.9
Sidi Rezegh
NOV.19, 25, DEC.7
BARDIA JAN.2
S.Azeiz
NOV.21
SIDI BARRANI
Gabr Saleh
Sollum
JAN.12
Capuzzo
B.Hakeim
El Gobi
S.Omar Nuovo
NOV.22
Halfaya
JAN.17
BuqBuq
Sidi Omar
Fort Steferzen
BRITISH PATROLS CROSS DESERT
B.Dignaish
A I C A
Fort Maddalena
BRITISH OFFENSIVE COMMENCED - NOV.18
LIBYAN DESERT PLATEAU
Magtuaed Saud
EGYPT
Y A
To Mersa Matruh
ESCARPMENT
Jarabub
BRITISH COLUMN CROSSES DESERT
Ghirba
DEC.13
Siwa Oasis

resistance in the El Agheila area which was being strenuously attacked. During these operations a German and Italian army of more than 100,000 men had been notably defeated, and much of its equipment had been destroyed. Axis air losses during the first six weeks alone amounted to 467 aircraft against a British loss of 195.

JAPANESE SUCCESS IN CHINA. On Christmas Day, after resisting Japanese attacks for seven days, and rejecting three demands to surrender, the British colony of Hong Kong capitulated. Under the leadership of Sir Mark Young, the Governor, the garrison of British, Canadian and Indian troops, had fought heroically against overwhelming odds and continual artillery and air bombardment. The decision to surrender was only taken after important reservoirs had fallen into enemy hands and there was one day's supply of water left. The picture shows Japanese artillery in action in the outskirts of the city just before the garrison surrendered.

ATTACK ON ENEMY SHIPPING. On 27 December British forces landed on the coast of Norway at Maaloy and Vaagso Islands. Coast defences were silenced by British warships and bombers, and commandos were landed under cover of smoke screens. The operation resulted in the destruction of 15,560 tons of enemy shipping in addition to munition dumps, oil tanks and military stores. The pictures show : above, an oil factory at Vaagso ablaze after having been blown up by British sappers ; and below, a commando on a height overlooking Maaloy, where the entire garrison were either killed or taken prisoner. All the British ships returned safely.

GERMAN REVERSE IN THE CRIMEA. On 30 December Russian forces of the Caucasus Command, with strong support from the Black Sea Fleet and the Red Air Force, crossed the Kerch Straits into the Crimea, and after fierce fighting captured the towns of Kerch and Feodosia which had been occupied by the Germans in November. Cossack troops, who played a prominent part in these operations are seen (above) bringing up machine guns in face of heavy enemy artillery fire; and, below, waiting to attack an enemy blockhouse.

JAPANESE ADVANCE IN LUZON. On 31 December the American and Filipino forces, faced with over-whelmingly superior numbers of enemy troops, backed by tanks and dive bombers, were forced to evacuate Manila and Cavite and fall back to shorter lines. The island fortress of Corregidor, at the entrance to Manila Bay, continued to hold out. Japanese forces entered the capital (above) at 3 p.m. where they found all military stores destroyed. Below, the city of Intramuros, the old part of Manila, is seen ablaze after an air attack.

CHINESE VICTORY IN HUNAN. On 1 January the Japanese armies launched an offensive against Changsha, capital of Hunan, an important centre on the railway from Manchuria and Korea via Peking and Hankow to Canton. Japanese control of this vital town would have considerably facilitated transport of troops and war material to the Burma and Malaya fronts. Into this offensive the enemy threw 50,000 men, but the seasoned Chinese troops, under General Hsueh Yueh, succeeded in encircling a large portion of this force between the

Liuyang and Laotao Rivers where they inflicted enormous casualties on the Japanese. By the 5th the offensive had collapsed and the Japanese armies were in disorderly retreat. Altogether it was estimated that casualties of upwards of 35,000 men had been inflicted upon the enemy. The pictures show: top, left, Chinese infantry launching an attack on the encircled Japanese; below, right, Japanese troops advancing to attack during the early stages of the offensive. Japanese bombing attacks on Changsha are shown in the other two pictures.

JUNGLE WARFARE IN MALAYA. After carrying out landings in Northern Malaya early in December, the Japanese launched strong assaults on the British positions with light tanks and armoured vehicles, supported by masses of dive bombers. Further landings on the coast behind the British lines seriously threatened the defenders' flanks and forced them to carry out a series of tactical withdrawals in face of strong enemy pressure. By these tactics the Japanese gained control of the northern aerodromes and were able to concentrate overwhelming air superiority on all sectors of the front. By 17 December, Penang, on the west coast, had been

evacuated, and on the 29th the tin mining town of Ipoh was in Japanese hands. On 7 January the enemy launched a strong offensive in Lower Perak in which he used 12-ton tanks to crash his way through the British lines. As a result Kuala Lampur, capital of the Federated Malay States, was evacuated on the 11th. The pictures show: left, enemy tanks and motor vehicles on a jungle road on fire after being engaged by anti-tank guns; in the lower picture one of the crew lies dead beside his tank; right, above, British anti-tank gunners firing at enemy tanks over open sights, and, (below), a close-up view of a knocked-out tank with its dead crew by its side.

AXIS GARRISONS SURRENDER. The town of Bardia, which had been occupied by the New Zealanders on 22 November and reoccupied by the enemy on 1 December, surrendered unconditionally to British and Imperial forces on 2 January after a brilliant attack in which Polish and Free French forces took part. Over 7,000 Axis prisoners were taken, including Major-General Schmidt, administrative head of the Afrika Korps. British casualties were only sixty killed and 300 wounded. Having reduced Bardia, the British forces turned

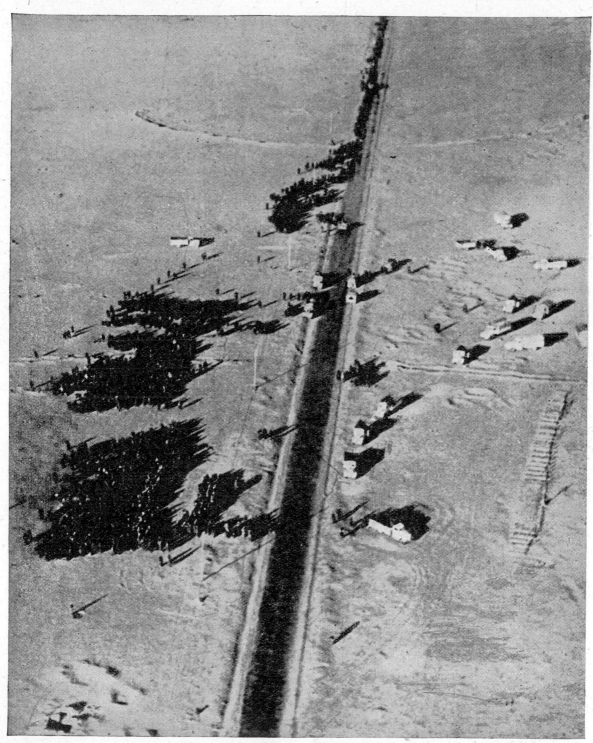

their attention to the strong enemy positions covering Helafaya, last remaining pocket of enemy resistance in E. Cyrenaica.   On the 12th they captured Sollum and five days later Helafaya itself surrendered after putting up a stiff resistance.   Here a further 5,500 prisoners were taken, together with large quantities of guns and war material.   The pictures show: above, Axis prisoners outside Bardia waiting to be taken to prison camps; top, left, some of the 300 prisoners captured at Sollum; below, left, the surrender of the Axis force at Helafaya.

RUSSIANS RECAPTURE MOJAISK

19 JANUARY, 1942

Although the Russians had succeeded in driving the Germans out of Klin, Kalinin and Kaluga thereby removing the German pincer threat to Moscow from the north and south, the enemy forces in Mojaisk, in the centre, fought desperately to retain this important position which they had won at great cost on 6 December. Mojaisk was the bastion of the German winter defence line on the Moscow front and the only remaining spearhead of the former German positions near the capital. So long as it remained in enemy hands the immediate threat to the city remained. Moreover, it would have provided an excellent jumping-off point for future offensive action by the enemy against Moscow. During January, Russian pressure on this vital town steadily increased. On the 14th the town of Medyn, an important point in the enemy defensive system, was captured, and on the 18th Vereya, only thirteen miles from Mojaisk was taken after fierce fighting. On the following day the assault on Mojaisk was launched. Soviet Guards and strong armoured units stormed the town and after bitter street fighting in which the Germans defended themselves house by house, the remnants of the German forces, covered by rearguards of panzer troops, beat a hurried retreat towards Vyasma, harried by Russian cavalry and ski-troops, and ceaselessly attacked by "Stormovik" dive bombers. It was estimated that at least three divisions, including some of the finest troops in the German Army, were wiped out during the fighting for Mojaisk, the town which Hitler had ordered the defenders to hold at all costs. The picture, specially drawn by Feliks Topolski, shows a lorryload of Russian infantry that has just been rushed up to the front line preparatory to the final assault on the town. They are escorted by cavalry, whose manœuvrability over the snow-covered ground made them particularly effective in winter warfare. On the left, a heavy tank, followed by white-clad infantry, is moving forward towards its objective.

ASSAULT ON MOJAISK. Hooded Russian infantry, clad from head to foot in white to make them invisible against the snow, are here seen approaching Mojaisk during the final stages of the Russian assault on the town.

FIGHTING BEGINS IN BURMA. On 20 January, Japanese and Thai forces crossed the frontier into Burma, and fighting occurred north of Myawaddi, sixty miles east of Moulmein. In face of a numerically superior enemy the British forces were obliged to fall slowly back towards Moulmein. The enemy used strong air

forces to support his offensive, but fighters of the R.A.F. and the American Volunteer Group inflicted heavy
losses on the raiders.   Above, Japanese infantry, some of whom are equipped with cycles, are seen crossing
a river by a temporary bridge, the main structure having been destroyed by the British before they retired.

AUSTRALIA THREATENED. After a Japanese landing on Sarawak on 16 December, the British forces withdrew, on 1 January, to Dutch Borneo, where they joined up with Netherlands troops. On the 10th, however, the enemy landed at Tarakan, Dutch Borneo, and also on North Celebes. The oil installations at Tarakan were destroyed by the Dutch before they were forced to surrender on the 13th. On 22 January, after fresh enemy landings, the oil wells at Balikpapan, on the east coast, were destroyed to prevent them falling into enemy hands. On the same day landings were carried out on New Ireland and at Rabaul, capital of New

Britain, in the Bismarck Archipelago, thereby threatening New Guinea and bringing the war dangerously close to Australia. On the 23rd, heavy Japanese air raids were made on Lae, New Guinea, which was evacuated after the attack. The pictures on the left show: above, blazing hangars at the aerodrome at Salamaua, not far from Lae, after a heavy Japanese raid; and below, the Balikpapan oil wells blazing furiously after their voluntary destruction by the Dutch forces. The radioed pictures above, show: top, a Japanese landing party somewhere in the Pacific; and below, warships putting up a smoke screen to cover a landing by Japanese forces.

U.S. TROOPS AT BATTLE PRACTICE. On 26 January the first American troops to land in Britain since 1917 disembarked at a Northern Ireland port. They formed the vanguard of the American Expeditionary Force to Europe, and they had been convoyed safely across the Atlantic by British and U.S. warships. After disembarking, the troops marched to camps that had been prepared in readiness for their arrival, and before long they were getting into battle trim by strenuous manœuvres over rough country. The pictures show: above, U.S. gun teams practising with British artillery; and below, infantry following up heavy General Grant tanks during a mock attack.

RETREAT TO SINGAPORE. After a fighting retreat in face of a numerically superior enemy who had almost undisputed control of the air, all the British and Empire forces on the Malayan mainland were withdrawn to Singapore Island on the night of 30-31 January. The operation was covered by a stand south of Kulai by Argyll and Sutherland and Gordon Highlanders, who inflicted heavy casualties on the enemy. After the withdrawal the Causeway linking the island with the mainland was blown up. The map shows the stages of the Japanese advance, with insets of Malaya in relation to surrounding territory, and Singapore Island.

U.S. NAVY HITS BACK.   On 1 February a brilliant surprise attack was carried out on Japanese naval and air bases in the Marshall and Gilbert Islands by a U.S. force of aircraft carriers supported by cruisers and destroyers.   Heavy damage was caused to enemy ships and harbour installations and many aircraft were destroyed on the ground.   The Japanese losses amounted to one light cruiser, a destroyer, two ocean-going submarines, a 17,000 ton liner, three 10,000 ton tankers, five 5,000 ton cargo ships, two fleet auxiliaries and two minesweepers, amounting in all to some 100,000 tons.   In addition at least eight more ships, amounting

to about 50,000 tons, were severely damaged. Thirty-eight enemy aircraft were destroyed in combat for a loss of eleven U.S. machines. The air bases at Taroa, Wotje, Roy and Enybor were wiped out. No U.S. vessel was lost. The pictures, taken during these operations, show: top, a U.S. naval aircraft over Wotje Atoll, the columns of smoke come from ammunition and fuel dumps that have been set on fire. Left, an American cruiser and aircraft carrier during the action; the latter has just been narrowly missed by a Japanese bomb. Right, the flight deck of one of the aircraft carriers with its aircraft lined up on the deck ready to take off.

LANDINGS ON SINGAPORE ISLAND. After the British and Empire forces retired across the Causeway from Johore Bahru to Singapore Island on 31 January, there was a brief lull in the offensive during which time the Japanese forces on the mainland re-organized for the final assault on the island fortress. Meanwhile the island's batteries were in constant action, firing across the narrow straits at the heights south-east of Johore Bahru and at the approaches to the Causeway, where the enemy were massing and bringing up transport. In reply Japanese bombers carried out numerous high level and dive bombing attacks on the British positions and upon the city of Singapore itself, where they caused considerable damage to life and property. Just before midnight on 8 February the main assault began. It was preceded by a violent artillery and air bombardment which lasted throughout the day after which Japanese infantry in great force made landings from special assault barges on a ten-mile front between Sungei Kranji and Pasir Laba, on the north-west of the Island. British, Australian, Indian and Chinese troops offered strong resistance, but were pushed back in some places with the result that there was some enemy infiltration eastwards. On the 9th fresh enemy landings of troops and light armoured vehicles forced the defenders to make further withdrawals, harassed all the time by high and low level air attacks by enemy fighters and bombers. British aircraft on the island were constantly in action, but were able to offer little effective protection to their troops in face of the overwhelming Japanese air superiority. By the 12th fierce fighting was taking place in the neighbourhood of the racecourse, two miles north-west of the city, and the reservoirs, the only source of Singapore's water supply, were seriously threatened. The pictures show: above, a Malayan mother sitting among the debris of a Singapore street, crying bitterly at the loss of her child, whose naked body lies in the road where it was struck down by a fragment from a Japanese bomb during a raid on Singapore. Left, above, Japanese light tanks at the Johore end of the Causeway; below, Japanese lorries crossing an improvised bridge to Singapore Island, built to replace the damaged Causeway.

SIX "SWORDFISH" IN SUICIDE ATTACK. At 11 a.m. on 12 February reconnaissance aircraft reported that a German naval squadron consisting of the 26,000 ton battle cruisers "Scharnhorst" and "Gneisenau" and the 10,000 ton cruiser "Prinz Eugen," accompanied by destroyers, torpedo boats, E-boats and minesweepers, and heavily escorted by fighter aircraft, were approaching the Strait of Dover from the westward. Coastal craft of the Dover Command, together with six "Swordfish" torpedo-carrying aircraft of the Naval Air Arm,

strongly escorted by R.A.F. fighters, were immediately sent out to engage the enemy. In conditions of bad visibility, and in face of a terrific barrage from the battleships and their escorts, the "Swordfish" pressed home their attacks at mast-height, and at least one hit was scored. Not one of the "Swordfish" returned, and of the eighteen men who flew them, only five were saved. The picture, by Norman Wilkinson, P.R.I., shows the "Swordfish" diving to the attack, undeterred by the tremendous A.A. screen put up by the German battleships.

GERMAN WARSHIPS' CHANNEL DASH. After the attack by the "Swordfish," powerful British air forces, including torpedo-carrying "Beauforts," kept up incessant attacks on the enemy ships for five hours. Low clouds and bad visibility made results difficult to ascertain, but the pilots were confident that each of the main enemy units was hit. The enemy themselves admitted the loss of a patrol vessel and a large torpedo boat. At 3.45 British destroyers and M.T.B.s attacked the enemy off the Dutch coast with torpedoes under very heavy fire from the Germans. No British warship was lost, but H.M.S. "Worcester" sustained some damage. When last seen the enemy squadron was making for the Heligoland Bight at reduced speed. Apart from the six

"Swordfish," British air losses amounted to twenty bombers and sixteen fighters against a German loss of eighteen. Altogether some 600 British aircraft took part in the engagement. The "Scharnhorst" and the "Gneisenau" had been at Brest for more than ten months during which time they had been constantly attacked by aircraft of the R.A.F. (see pages 86-87), and more than 4,000 tons of bombs had been dropped on them. British losses in these sorties amounted to forty-three aircraft and 247 men. The pictures show, top, a German destroyer, with a low-flying air umbrella, during the Channel dash; left, the "Scharnhorst" and "Gneisenau," with escorting vessels, at the beginning of the voyage, and right, British destroyers dashing in to the attack.

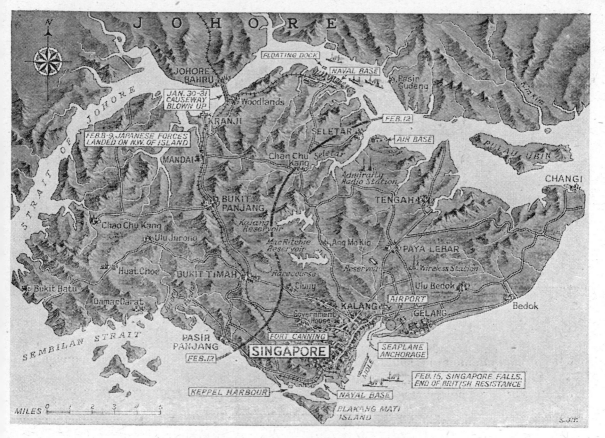

FALL OF SINGAPORE
15 FEBRUARY, 1942

By 13 February the Japanese forces on Singapore Island had reached the neighbourhood of the MacRitchie Reservoir, and fierce fighting was taking place there and at Ang Mo Kio village, to the north-east (see map). Farther south strong pressure was being exerted at Pasir Panjang, where the enemy were throwing masses of men and tanks into the battle in a desperate effort to take the city by storm. The defenders put up a magnificent resistance, and their artillery, which was firing at the rate of 400 rounds per hour, inflicted severe casualties on the enemy. On the 14th, however, in spite of strong counter-attacks, the enemy occupied the Naval Base and penetrated the outskirts of the city. In a telegram to London on that day the Governor of Malaya, Sir Shenton Thomas, reported that a million people in Singapore were concentrated within a radius of three miles and that the city's water supplies were badly damaged and unlikely to last more than twenty-four hours.

The end came on 15 February. In the evening four British officers bearing the flag of truce presented themselves at the Japanese Army H.Q., and at 7 p.m. Lieutenant-General Percival, the British commander accepted General Yamashita's demands for unconditional surrender. Cease fire was sounded at 10 p.m. The Japanese formally occupied Singapore on the 16th, and on the same day they announced that in future it would be known as Shonan (Light of the South).

Thus ended the campaign in Malaya. It had lasted for seventy days and had been fought against a numerically superior enemy who, from the outset, had had almost undisputed control of the air. The Japanese proved themselves to be masters of the art of infiltration and the defenders had constantly to withdraw in order to prevent their flanks being turned. The fighting on Singapore Island itself was carried on in face of almost hopeless odds. The island's aerodromes were constantly bombed and the few aircraft remaining were so outnumbered as to be almost useless. Nevertheless, the British and Imperial forces fought for eight days without a break until they were surrounded and helpless to defend themselves. The Japanese claimed that they had taken 60,000 prisoners, made up of 32,000 Indians, 15,000 British, and 13,000 Australians.

The pictures, left, show, top, a damaged British ship in the docks at Singapore during a bombing attack, and bottom, burning buildings and warehouses on the waterfront. In the centre picture Japanese infantry and tanks are seen in action in the outskirts of the city; the curious cloven shoes worn by the soldiers are used to facilitate climbing up trees in jungle fighting.

BATTLE FOR SINGAPORE. The landings on Singapore Island were carried out under cover of darkness by Japanese troops who had crossed the Johore Strait in barges. On reaching the shore they waded through the mangrove swamps and infiltrated through the British lines, thereby forcing the defenders to reform further inland. These operations were strongly supported by Japanese aircraft, which dived low over the island bombing and machine gunning the British and Imperial troops. Some idea of the confused nature of the fighting may be

gathered by the illustration, specially drawn for this book by T. C. Dugdale, A.R.A. It depicts the early stages of the fighting and shows mass British artillery in action near the Causeway (seen in background). The flashes from the mainland come from enemy batteries situated along the coast, from which point they maintained an almost non-stop bombardment of the British positions. Heavy high altitude and dive bombing helped to add confusion to the scene. The aerial supremacy enjoyed by the enemy to a large extent dictated the course of the fighting.

W.I.P.3—E

FALL OF PEGU. On 30 January the Japanese forces in Burma occupied Moulmein and the British retired to the west bank of the Salween river. On 10 February, however, the enemy crossed the river north-west of Martaban and after fierce fighting occupied the town. Farther north other attempts to cross the river in the Paan area were repulsed, but on the 15th, the British were withdrawn to the line of the Bilin river after evacuating Thaton. Here strong counter-attacks, in which the R.A.F., the Indian Air Force and the American Volunteer Group gave valuable support, slowed down the Japanese advance, but on the 22nd a fresh attack was mounted by the enemy who

forced a crossing of the Bilin and made heavy assaults on a bridgehead on the east bank of the Sittang river, the next obstacle in their way. The town of Pegu, forty miles north of Rangoon, fell, and the railway from Rangoon to Mandalay and the road to China were thereby cut. The pictures show: above, left, General Yamashita, Japanese commander in Malaya and Burma, on a tour of occupied territory; and right, Japanese horse transport passing through a Burmese village; below, left, a Japanese tank column crossing a river over an emergency bridge built to replace one destroyed by the British; and right, Buffalo fighters of the R.A.F. taking off from a Burmese airfield.

RUSSIAN ATTEMPT TO RELIEVE LENINGRAD. On 23 February, the twenty-fourth anniversary of the creation of the Red Army, Russian forces launched an offensive on the Central Front and on the same day the High Command announced the capture of Dorogobuzh, fifty miles east of Smolensk. Farther north, where the Russians were striving desperately to break the German ring round Leningrad, Soviet troops, on the 24th, successfully accomplished the encirclement of the German 16th Army at Staraya Russa, ten miles south of Lake

Ilmen. After the refusal of the German commander to surrender, the Russians began an attack in which two German infantry divisions and the crack S.S. "Death's Head" Division were smashed and 12,000 Germans were killed. Nevertheless, the enemy, heartened by promises of airborne reinforcements, clung desperately to their positions. The pictures show: left, German infantry waiting in the snow beside their guns in readiness for an expected Russian attack; and right, Russian sappers clearing a passage for their troops through enemy wire.

**BURMESE CAPITAL THREAT-
ENED.** In view of the proxi-
mity of Japanese forces to Rangoon, a curfew was imposed
and a military governor ap-
pointed, on 25 February, in
order to prevent looting. On
the same day the R.A.F. and the
American Volunteer Group
scored a notable success
by shooting down thirty Japanese bombers attempting to raid
the capital. Meanwhile, in India,
the evacuation of part of the
Chittagong district, on the
shores of the Bay of Bengal, was
carried out as a precautionary
measure. The pictures show:
above, natives interestedly examining bomb damage in a
main Rangoon street following a heavy Japanese air raid;
and left, a grief-stricken Bur-
man, whose wife has just been
killed by a fragment from a
Japanese bomb, clutching his
little child closely to his side.

British raid on Bruneval

ENEMY RADIOLOCATION STATION WRECKED. On the night of 27-28 February the Army, Navy and R.A.F. carried out a combined attack on an important German radiolocation station at Bruneval, on the French coast twelve miles north of Le Havre. Parachute troops dropped by R.A.F. bombers carried out the demolition, despite heavy enemy resistance, and the station was entirely wrecked. Infantry units landed from the sea by light naval forces covered the embarkation of the airborne forces. Heavy casualties were inflicted on the Germans and a number of prisoners were taken. No British ships or aircraft were lost. The pictures show: above, British parachute troops about to enter their aircraft, and below, landing barges returning to their bases after the raid.

PACIFIC THEATRE OF WAR. This map shows the progress of the war in the Pacific from the outbreak of hostilities to the Japanese occupation of the Andaman Islands on 23 March, 1942. During that time the whole of Malaya had been overrun, Borneo, Java, Sumatra and Celebes had been occupied, and fighting was in progress in New Guinea where Japanese landings had taken place after the enemy occupation of the adjoining islands of New Britain and New Ireland. American and Filipino forces in the Philippines were still resisting the enemy who had

PRINCIPAL NAVAL BASES

BRITISH • AMERICAN • RUSSIAN • DUTCH • JAPANESE

MAIN OILFIELDS   TERRITORY OCCUPIED BY JAPANESE

gained control of the greater part of the islands. The U.S. naval bases of Guam and Wake had fallen early in the campaign, but Midway Island continued to repel all enemy attempts to take it. On the Burmese front British forces were retreating before a numerically superior enemy in the direction of Mandalay. The entry of Japan into the war cut the Far Eastern supply route to Russia, whilst their expansion south-eastwards presented a potential threat to the supply lines between America and the Antipodes. Shipping in the Indian Ocean was also threatened.

ATTACK ON BILLANCOURT. On the night of 3 March the R.A.F. carried out an attack on the huge Renault works at Billancourt on the south-west outskirts of Paris, which were engaged in making and repairing tanks, transport vehicles and aeroplane engines for Germany. A great weight of bombs was dropped, and the pictures reproduced on this page provide ample evidence of the success of the attack. They show: left, the wreckage of the modelling department (in foreground) and destroyed workshops (centre). Above, what was left of the tank and motor workshops; note the lorries parked along the roadways on each side.

RUINS OF A RENAULT WORKSHOP. After the R.A.F. bombing attack on the Renault factory near Paris,
German propaganda put out the story that most of the damage had fallen on civilian and workers' homes. This
was disproved shortly after the raid by a remarkable series of photographs, one of which is reproduced above,

that was smuggled out of France. This proves the deadly accuracy of the R.A.F.'s bombing and shows a tangled mass of girders and machinery, all that was left of one of the factory's main workshops. In this building crankshafts, valves and motors were made. The loss of this factory was a serious blow to German war production.

GERMAN SUPPLY BASE CAPTURED. On 5 March Soviet forces under General Golubov recaptured Yukhnov, 125 miles east of Smolensk, an important rail centre and supply base for the German armies on the Central Front. The town, which was protected by a formidable double row of fortifications, fell after a fierce struggle lasting several days, during which Soviet troops fought their way through the battered streets and engaged in house-to-house fighting. The pictures show: above, a Soviet Scouts Company, the first to enter the town, advancing cautiously through the ruined streets; and below, camouflaged infantry engaged in mopping-up operations.

DAYLIGHT ATTACK ON MATFORD WORKS. Five days after the heavy night attack on the Renault factory, a small formation of American-built "Boston" light bombers carried out a daring low-level daylight attack on the Matford works at Poissy, ten miles north-west of Paris, which was producing twenty lorries a day for the German Army. The picture taken from one of the attacking bombers during the height of the raid, shows bombs bursting in the centre of the factory. Hits were also scored on the rows of parked lorries which can be seen at the back of the building. Never before had British bombers penetrated so far into occupied France in daylight.

FALL OF RANGOON. As a result of the isolation of part of the British forces at Pegu, and Japanese landings on the Irrawaddy Delta, the city of Rangoon, capital of Burma, was evacuated on 7 March, and on the following day the Japanese entered the town. The British forces, despite heavy casualties, remained intact after the Pegu fighting and withdrew into Central Burma with the object of linking up with the Chinese armies farther north. Before the evacuation of Rangoon the "scorched earth" policy was thoroughly carried out; all dock installations, oil refineries and machinery that could not be removed were systematically destroyed. The photograph, taken from one of the last ships to leave the port, shows the dense clouds of oil smoke rising from the Burma Oil Company's warehouses

that have been set on fire to prevent them falling into enemy hands. On the same day as he evacuation of Rangoon, Japanese forces who had landed in Java on 1 March occupied Batavia, the capital, and three days later Surabaya, the Dutch naval base, and the city of Bandoeng, were in enemy hands, the la.ter having surrendered to prevent an aerial massacre of the civilian population. With the fall of these towns the fighting in Java came to an end. The gallant Dutch had lost most of their navy in trying to prevent the enemy landngs, and their air force was no match for the masses of aircraft the enemy were able to throw into the battle. The Japanese, who used at least ten divisions in the fighting, claimed that 93,000 Dutch and 5,000 British, Australian and American troops had surrendered.

WAR APPROACHES
On 8 March the Japanese took another step nearer to Australia by landing in force at Salamaua and Lae, New Guinea. Two days later a third landing was carried out at Finsch Harbour, seventy miles east of Salamaua. Aircraft of the R.A.A.F. and the U.S. Air Force heavily attacked the invaders and carried out non-stop raids on Lae and the aerodrome at Salamaua where many enemy aircraft were destroyed. On 11 March an enemy invasion fleet was sighted heading in the direction of Port Moresby, and Australian and U.S. bombers, including many huge "Flying Fortresses," went out to attack it. In the action that followed the enemy fleet was broken up and dispersed and thirteen transports were sunk or damaged. Further raids were carried out on the Japanese-occupied port of Rabaul and the aerodrome of Gasmata, in New Britain. On 17 March General

AUSTRALIA'S SHORES. Douglas MacArthur, former commander of the U.S. forces in the Philippines, arrived in Australia by air to take over supreme command of the land, naval and air forces in the South-west Pacific. With the announcement of General MacArthur's appointment it was made known that for the past two months a steady stream of U.S. soldiers and airmen had been pouring into Australia and that U.S. troops were stationed at Darwin ready to repel any attacks on the Commonwealth which, according to General Brett, Deputy Supreme Commander, could and would be held against the largest scale Japanese attack. The pictures show: above, a U.S. convoy, with naval escort, proceeding towards its destination in the Pacific; left, American soldiers wearing lifebelts, en route to Australia; and right, war material being loaded aboard a U.S. ship bound for Australia.

PORT ENGINE
FALLING INTO
SEA

ALLIED AIR SUCCESSES IN THE PACIFIC. On 18 March the U.S. Navy Department gave details of successes obtained by American and Australian airmen in operations against the Japanese forces invading New Guinea. These included the sinking of two heavy cruisers, damage to three light cruisers, five transports gutted by fire and beached as well as damage to other miscellaneous craft. In all twenty-three enemy ships were sunk or damaged for the loss of one Allied aircraft. On the 19th considerable Japanese forces in New Guinea were seen advancing across the island in a south-westerly direction, but attacks by U.S. bombers on Lae and on Rabaul, where a heavy cruiser was sunk, so interfered with the enemy's plans that he was obliged, at least temporarily, to call it to a halt. Tokyo admitted that at Rabaul alone they had sustained 7,000 casualties. The pictures show the end of a Japanese twin-engined bomber that attempted to attack a U.S. naval force in the Pacific. It is seen over a U.S. destroyer (1) shortly before it received a direct hit on its port engine, which broke off and fell into the sea (2). The aircraft immediately went into a steep dive (3) and crashed into the sea in flames (4). The crew of three perished.

MALTA CONVOY GETS THROUGH. On 22 March a convoy carrying important supplies to Malta from Alexandria, and protected by a naval force comprising a 6-inch gun cruiser, A.A. cruisers and destroyers under the command of Rear-Admiral P. L. Vian, was attacked by four Italian cruisers. These were driven off, but later in the day the 35,000-ton Italian battleship "Littorio," with two 8-inch gun and four 6-inch gun cruisers and destroyers approached the convoy. Despite the great disparity in numbers the British force immediately attacked. Three destroyers closed to within three miles of the "Littorio" and delivered a torpedo attack in which a direct hit was scored. The "Littorio" was also hit by a salvo from a British cruiser which set her on fire aft. In addition severe damage was inflicted on an 8-inch gun cruiser, after which the enemy force withdrew in confusion. The British

force escaped serious damage by the use of smoke screens, although some damage was suffered by a cruiser and three destroyers. Throughout the 22nd and 23rd heavy air attacks were made on the convoy by some 150 bombers and one merchant ship was sunk. The remainder reached port safely on the 24th. The pictures, taken during the action, show: (1), A British destroyer, with guns blazing, closing in to attack the enemy; (2) heavy A.A. fire from British ships bursting round an enemy torpedo bomber just before it was shot down into the sea; (3) a destroyer emerging from a smoke screen at full speed to launch her torpedoes against the Italian warships; (4) a destroyer putting down a smoke screen to protect the British ships and confuse the enemy gunners; in the foreground a British light cruiser elevates its guns ready for action; (5) the convoy sailing safely on after the attack was beaten off.

BRITISH AND CHINESE
After the fall of Rangoon Lieutenant-General Sir Harold Alexander took over command in Burma from General Hutton. Under his leadership the British forces withdrew northwards and on 12 March linked up with a powerful Chinese force that had marched 800 miles from Yunnan. On the 19th the enemy began to push northwards towards Toungoo, on the Sittang, and towards Prome, on the Irrawaddy, with the result that the British were obliged to evacuate Tharawaddy, on the Rangoon-Prome railway, on the 20th. At Pyu, thirty-five miles south of Toungoo, the Japanese came up against strong Chinese resistance, but by an outflanking movement they managed to capture

CONTACT IN BURMA the aerodrome north of Toungoo and cut the Toungoo-Mandalay road, and on the 25th they occupied Kyungon, north-west of the town, thereby almost encircling the Chinese. The Chinese held Toungoo against strong enemy attacks until the 31st, when they fought their way out of the trap and rejoined their main forces to the north-west. The pictures above show: left, Chinese forces passing through a Burmese village on their way to the battlefront; and right, digging anti-tank ditches in the jungle. Below, left, a camouflaged Chinese sniper is seen picking off enemy stragglers; and right, a lightly-clad infantryman is doubling through the jungle during a surprise attack.

RAID ON ENEMY HARBOUR INSTALLATIONS. In the early hours of 28 March a combined raid was carried out by light naval forces and commandos against the large dry dock and harbour installations at St. Nazaire. H.M. destroyer "Campbeltown," carrying five tons of high explosive in her specially stiffened bows, crashed through the harbour boom defences and charged the dock entrance at full speed. Such was the impact that she forced herself into the lock entrance as far as her bridge where, after most of her crew had been taken off by a

motor launch, she blew up.   Meanwhile commandos, who had been landed from launches, set about the work
of demolishing harbour works, including the pumping station and dock operating gear.   After completing their
tasks the British troops withdrew, but some were unable to get away owing to heavy enemy machine gun fire.   The
picture, specially drawn by Harold Forster, shows H.M.S. "Campbeltown" wedged firmly in the lock gates just
before she blew up.   Commandos are seen on the quayside making their way to their allotted objectives.

DAMAGE TO ST. NAZAIRE. The dry dock at St. Nazaire was the only one on the Atlantic coast capable of accommodating the German battleship "Tirpitz," and the damage done would, it was believed, seriously hamper enemy naval operations from that port. The Germans, who denied that any real damage had been caused, took great pains to prevent British reconnaissance aircraft from photographing the port after the raid, but several photographs were obtained in spite of heavy A.A. and fighter interference. The one reproduced above, although

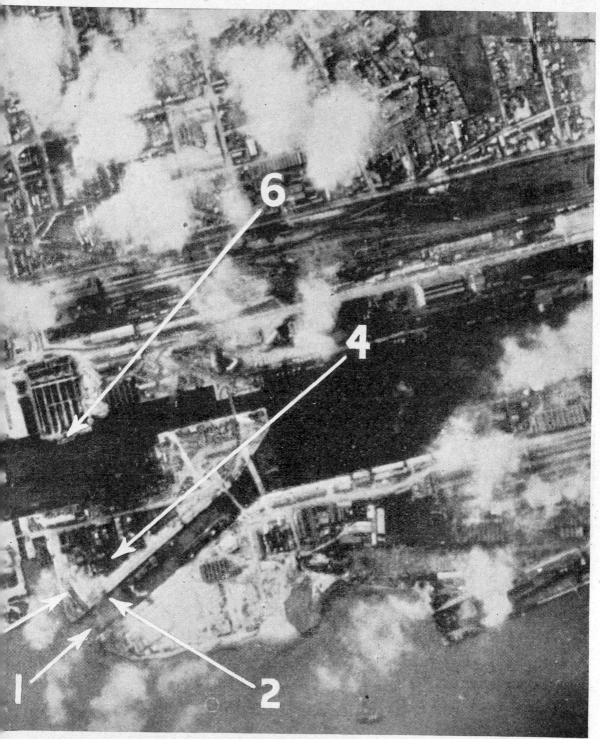

taken from a great height, shows that considerable damage was done. The numbers indicate: (1) The dry dock, the outer gate of which is now missing. It was here that H.M.S. Campbeltown blew up, although no trace of her remains. (2) Severe damage to the dock pump house; (3) Damage to the machine house for operating outer dock gate; (4) Two small sheds of the pump house completely demolished; (5) A five-bay building almost completely destroyed; (6) Damage to submarine pens under construction; (7) One end of a multi-bay building badly damaged.

LUEBECK BOMBED

28-29 MARCH, 1942

On the night of 28 March, a strong force of heavy bombers gave the Baltic port of Luebeck, thirty-five miles north of Hamburg, one of the heaviest bombings experienced by any German city so far. The port handles nearly all the traffic between Germany and Sweden, and large imports of iron ore and other raw materials pass through it on their way to feed Germany's war industries. In addition it was being used for the dispatch of military stores to Finland and to the German armies on the northern front, as well as to the army of occupation in Norway. The fact that it was also an important centre of U-boat construction and a training depot for submarine crews made it an extremely desirable target for the R.A.F.'s attention.

The attack was pressed home with great determination, and soon after it began, fires could be seen dotted all over the city. These rapidly spread until it looked as if there was only one huge fire. Very heavy damage was done, and it was estimated that about 1,500 houses were destroyed, mostly by fire. The photograph below shows a section of the centre of the city stretching over 1,500 yards. In this area the Central Electric Station, the Market Hall and the Reich Bank were all completely gutted, and a close inspection of the picture shows that there is scarcely a building in the whole area retaining its roof. The picture on the left shows chaos caused by British bombs in Breitstrasse.

GERMAN ATTACK FAILS. On 24 March the Germans launched the biggest attack on the Kalinin front since the Battle of Moscow. Its object was to relieve a deep salient in their lines near Rzhev, where two large bodies of their troops had been isolated. For this purpose they employed three divisions and large numbers of tanks and aircraft, but after five days' fighting they were obliged to call the attack off, having lost 2,500 men in killed alone. Meanwhile, near Staraya Russa, the Germans were still trying desperately to relieve their Sixteenth Army

which had now been reduced by almost half. On the Leningrad front the Red Army was trying hard to free the encircled city before the thaw cut the supply line across the ice on Lake Ladoga, whilst in the Ukraine they had reached the suburbs of Stalino, which they had lost on 20 October, and were fighting desperately to regain possession of the town. The picture shows a Russian battlefield after the tide of war has passed over it; dead bodies and burnt-out tanks litter the ground for miles around, whilst the snow casts a merciful white mantle alike over friend and foe.

THE WORLD AT WAR

At the end of 1941 the Axis Powers, with a combined population of 321 millions, and territory of their own amounting to rather more than one and a half million square miles, were opposed to the United Nations, whose population was 1,300 millions and whose territory covered nearly 30 million square miles. In the first two years of the war, however, the enemy had overrun territory in Europe amounting to almost a million square miles, and during the first few months of 1942 Japan, by her conquests in Burma and in the Pacific, had added another million square miles to the

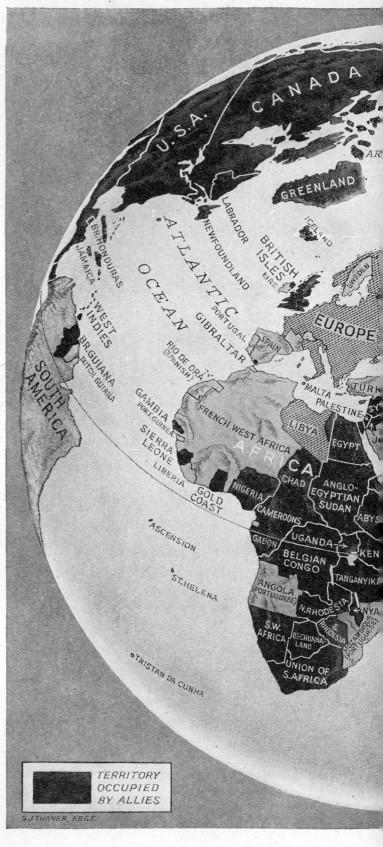

TERRITORY OCCUPIED BY ALLIES

S.J.TURNER, F.R.G.S.

Axis total. In round figures, therefore, the enemy, early in 1942, possessed rather more than $3\frac{1}{2}$ million square miles against an Allied total of 29 millions, which means that $32\frac{1}{2}$ million square miles out of a total earth land surface of $52\frac{1}{2}$ million square miles was directly involved in the struggle. The map, specially drawn by S. J. Turner, shows the disposition of the rival forces on this, the greatest battlefield the world has ever known. Inset are Hitler, Mussolini and Tojo (left), the men who plunged the world into chaos and bloodshed; and right, Churchill, Roosevelt, Stalin and Chiang-Kai-Shek who are leading the United Nations in the world crusade against dictatorship and tyranny.

CONVOY FOILS GERMAN ATTACK. On 27 March a convoy carrying war supplies to the Russian port of Murmansk was attacked by German dive bombers north-west of Tromsö. This was beaten off by aircraft of the Naval Air Arm and by gunfire from the naval escort, but on the 30th the enemy launched two determined attacks with destroyers and a third with aircraft and submarines. In these actions the enemy lost one destroyer and three U-boats. Russian fighters from Murmansk co-operated with the naval escort in driving off the enemy bombers during the last attack. Some damage was suffered by H.M.S.S. "Eclipse" and "Trinidad," but both ships reached port safely. The pictures show two aspects of a Nazi attack on a Russia-bound convoy. Above, an enemy torpedo aircraft is seen swooping low over an escorting destroyer; and below, a direct hit with bombs on one of the ships.

FIGHTING RETREAT IN BURMA. After evacuating Toungoo the Chinese forces, now reorganized north of the town, launched a determined counter-attack, and on 2 April succeeded in recapturing Kyungon, which the enemy had occupied on 25 March. Meanwhile, on the Irrawaddy front, Japanese forces in considerable strength penetrated the British positions south of Prome and on 2 April, after an all-night battle, occupied the town. This brought them to within 120 miles of the important oilfields at Yenang Yaung, which was one of their main objectives. On 3 April Japanese aircraft bombed Mandalay in the heaviest raid of the Far East war to date. It was estimated that about two-thirds of the business area was destroyed and that between 2,000 and 3,000 people were killed and thousands injured. The picture shows bomb damage in a section of the Moslem residential quarter after the raid.

MALTA DEFIES THE LUFTWAFFE. The island of Malta, which stands on the direct sea route from Italy to North Africa and from which attacks were carried out by British aircraft on Axis convoys carrying reinforcements to General Rommel in Libya, was the subject of almost non-stop attacks by German and Italian bombers. During April the enemy launched a particularly heavy offensive in order to ground British aircraft whilst his convoys made the dangerous crossing to North Africa, and on the 7th, Malta had its two thousandth alert since war began.

On this day alone the enemy employed about 500 aircraft on attacks on the island. According to reports from Valletta about 4,200 houses had been destroyed in the raids to date, as well as the island's Opera House, the Church and Monastery of the Sacred Heart, the Capuchin Convent Church, and the Chapel of our Lady of Lourdes. The pictures show: left, bomb damage in the centre of Valletta; right, above, a picture taken by the R.A.F. Film Unit showing bombs bursting on Valletta harbour; below, bomb bursts on the island, as seen from a raiding aircraft.

STRATEGIC IMPORTANCE OF THE INDIAN OCEAN

APRIL, 1942

By their occupation of the whole of the Malay Archipelago, completed on 17 April by the surrender of Dutch and Imperial forces in Sumatra, the Japanese gained for themselves valuable naval and air bases astride important British shipping routes from which they could hamper Allied movements between the Pacific and Indian Oceans. Moreover, by occupying the Andaman Islands in the Bay of Bengal on 23 March they obtained a useful advance naval anchorage at Port Blair from which their aircraft carriers and light naval forces could operate in the Indian Ocean.

It was from this base that a strong force of carriers and other naval units set out early in April to bomb the British naval base at Trincomalee, Ceylon. The attack was carried out on the 9th by a strong bomber force with fighter escorts. Twenty-one of the raiders were destroyed. In this action the 10,000-ton British cruisers "Dorsetshire" and "Cornwall" were dive bombed and sunk. They had left the harbour at Trincomalee in order to avoid being caught at anchor by the enemy, but they were located by Japanese aircraft and subjected to an intense bombing attack. About 1,100 of their crews were saved. On the same day the old aircraft carrier "Hermes" was located about ten miles offshore from Trincomalee and sunk in the same way. A large proportion of her crew was picked up.

The extension of Japanese activities to the Indian Ocean constituted a grave threat to Allied communications in many parts of the world, for through this sea ran some of their most vital supply routes. The routes from Britain to India, and to Russia via the Persian Gulf, passed through these waters now that the passage through the Mediterranean via the Suez Canal had been closed, as did also the route for the supply of the British armies in Egypt and Syria. This route was now well within range of Japanese submarine attack. American ships carrying supplies to China and Russia via Australia, were also obliged to use this sea now that the shorter passages through the Pacific were controlled by the Japanese.

Naval supremacy in the Indian Ocean thus became of major importance in Allied war strategy, for any Japanese expansion westwards via the island groups stretching between Malaya and Africa would enable the enemy to harass, or even control vital sea lanes without which the sinews of war could not be carried to Allied forces in the Middle and Far Eastern theatres of war. It was for this reason that Britain took the drastic step of occupying Madagascar (see pages 188-191) and thereby forestalled Japanese intentions in that island. The map, specially drawn by S. J. Turner, F.R.G.S., gives the main shipping routes passing through the Indian Ocean and shows at a glance the vital importance of defending it against further Japanese encroachment.

TIBET

DELHI

INDIA
KARACHI
CALCUTTA

NEPAL
SADIYA
ASSAM ROAD

CHUNGKING
CHINA

SEA OF
JAPAN

KOBE

JAPAN
TOKYO
YOKOSUKA

SHANGHAI

BONIN IS.

AMAMIOSHIMA

BURMA ROAD
LASHIO
MANDALAY

TAINAN
HONG KONG
HAINAN
FORMOSA

PACIFIC OCEAN

SAIPAN

CHITTAGONG
BURMA

FRENCH INDO-CHINA

SOUTH CHINA
SEA
MANILA

GUAM

YAP

BAY OF BENGAL
MADRAS
ANDAMAN
ISLANDS
(BR.)
TRINCOMALEE

THAILAND
RANGOON
BANGKOK

CAMRANH
SAIGON

PHILIPPINE
ISLANDS

PELEW

CAROLINE
ISLANDS

COLOMBO
CEYLON

MALAYA

SINGAPORE

EQUATOR

SUMATRA

BORNEO

MACASSAR STRAIT

CELEBES

NEW
GUINEA

RABAUL

CHAGOS
ARCHIPELAGO
(BR.)

PALEMBANG

BATAVIA
SURABAYA

JAVA

TIMOR

THURSDAY I.
PORT
MORESBY

TO COLOMBO
MILES

COLOMBO TO FREMANTLE 3140 MILES

COCOS OR
KEELING IS.
(BR.)

DARWIN

CORAL
SEA

INDIAN

BROOME

CAIRNS
TOWNSVILLE

UEZ (BR.)

OCEAN

ROCKHAMPTON

AUSTRALIA

BRISBANE

FREMANTLE

ALBANY

ADELAIDE

SYDNEY
CANBERRA

TOWN TO MELBOURNE 5820 MILES

MELBOURNE

HOBART
TASMANIA

NEW
ZEALAND

KERGUELEN
(FR.)

HEARD
(BR.)

TERRITORY OCCUPIED BY ALLIES
TERRITORY OCCUPIED BY JAPANESE
OF AXIS IN AFRICA AND EUROPE
SHIPPING ROUTES OF ALLIES
SHIPPING ROUTES OF JAPANESE

END OF AN

On 9 April the U.S. and Filipino defences on the Batan Peninsula o Luzon were smashed by Japanese forces and an epic resistance which had lasted for four months was brought to an end. General Wainwright's forces on the island amounted to 36,800 men, nearly all of whom were killed or captured, but some of them, including 3,500 U.S. Marines succeeded in escaping to the island of Corregidor, which continued to hold out. Although outnumbered by six to one, the defending forces put up a magnificent resistance and succeeded in inflicting 60,000 casualties on

HEROIC DEFENCE. the enemy. It was only after they were physically exhausted by days and nights of fighting that they were finally compelled to give up. The pictures show : above, left, Japanese forces on the Peninsula passing blazing oil dumps that had been set on fire by the defenders before they surrendered, and right, some of the Japanese prisoners captured during the fighting. On the left two Japanese soldiers, killed in the fighting, are seen lying where they fell, and right, a Batan village after it had been blasted by enemy artillery and high-explosive bombs.

BRITAIN'S OFFER TO INDIA REJECTED. Charged with a special mission to present the British Government's plan to solve Indian Constitutional problems, Sir Stafford Cripps had arrived in New Delhi on 23 March. In the Prime Minister's words, Sir Stafford "did everything in human power" to ensure a successful conclusion to the negotiations, but the Congress of India now rejected Britain's proposals for a settlement. Britain's firm promise of Indian independence included a self-elected government for India after the War, but Congress made an uncompromising last-minute demand for the setting up of a National Government at once. Sir Stafford Cripps pointed out to Dr. Azad, the Congress President, that this demand implied absolute dictatorship of the majority, and would break all the pledges Britain had given to the great minorities of India. Although negotiations failed, Pandit Nehru, Congress Leader, declared: "We are not going to embarrass the British war effort in India." Above, Sir Stafford Cripps talks to some of the Sikh leaders during his visit. Below, Gandhi (in foreground), and Pandit Nehru (between the pillars) at a meeting of Congress

Pro-German government formed in Vichy

LAVAL COMES BACK TO POWER. On 14 April Berlin and Vichy announced that Laval would return to office and that Petain had decided to reconstitute the Vichy cabinet on a new basis. This reorganization was forced upon Petain by Hitler who, it was said, used the French prisoners of war in Germany and threats to starve the French people as bargaining weapons. With a pro-German head in Vichy, Hitler doubtless hoped to obtain the services of French workers for essential war work in German factories, and even to obtain the use of the French fleet, which had been disarmed under the armistice terms. The new cabinet, in which Laval held the post of Chief of Government, and the Ministries of Foreign Affairs, the Interior, and Information, was formed on the 17th, and on the same day President Roosevelt recalled Admiral Leahy, U.S. Ambassador to the Vichy Government, "for consultation." Petain retained the nominal title of Chief of State. Laval's appointment led to disturbances in Paris and Northern France, and on the 16th thirty-five German soldiers were killed in a troop train that was derailed near Caen. The picture above, doubtless a piece of German propaganda to prove the success of the new arrangement, shows French "volunteers" in German uniforms leaving Versailles for service on the Russian front. On the left, Marshal Petain and Laval are seen together shortly after the new government was formed.

"Hurricanes" attack Axis shipping

During the early months of 1942 aircraft of Fighter Command markedly increased their activities over the English Channel and German-occupied France. Several times a day large formations of "Hurricanes" and ' Spitfires" patrolled large areas of enemy territory, shooting up troop concentrations, bombing factories and attacking enemy fighters they encountered. These sweeps were not only useful from the standpoint of high-speed reconnaissance, but they also made it necessary for the enemy to keep a considerable fighter force in the West which could have been more profitably employed on the Russian front. The pictures reproduced on this page were taken by a squadron of "Hurricanes," armed with four cannon, during an offensive sweep over the Channel. They show four stages of an attack on an enemy ship.

In 1, taken by the leading "Hurricane" as it dived to the attack, the ship is seen just as the pilot pressed the gun button. No. 2, taken from the third "Hurricane," shows the second aircraft in the formation diving low over the ship to deliver its attack at mast level. As this machine pulls out of its dive the third "Hurricane" opens fire ; (3 and 4), and straddles the enemy with a long burst of cannon shells.

BRITISH RETREAT ALONG THE IRRAWADDY. After the fall of Prome on 2 April, the British forces in Burma withdrew northwards under heavy attack from Japanese aircraft. By 6 April they had reached Thayetmyo where, after demolishing the oil and cement installations, they took up defensive positions north of the town. A strong enemy attack, however, necessitated further withdrawal, and by the 13th the Japanese had occupied Migyaungwe, only forty miles from Yenang-Yaung, around which were situated the largest oilfields in Burma. This necessitated a Chinese withdrawal on the Sittang front from their positions north of Toungoo to the neighbourhood of Myohla. On the 16th, in face of continued enemy pressure, the British retired north of Magwe, at the same time destroying the Yenang-Yaung oil wells, seen blazing above, to prevent them falling into enemy hands. The work of demolition was successfully accomplished in spite of a heavy Japanese attack made with the object of preventing the work of destruction being carried out. A map of the fighting in Burma is given on page 185.

RAID ON DIESEL WORKS. On 17 April twelve "Lancasters"—Britain's most powerful four-engined bombers—took part in a spectacular and successful raid on the important German works at Augsburg, Bavaria, where half of the Diesel engines for the U-boat fleet are made, as well as numbers of tanks and armoured vehicles. In a daylight flight of 500 miles over enemy territory, the aircraft flew at a height of only 25 to 30 feet on the outward journey, skimming roof-tops and trees. Four "Lancasters" were shot down by enemy fighters south of Paris; the

rest reached their target, which they bombed with great effectiveness from 200 feet. Three more were shot down at Augsburg, but the remaining five reached home safely. Great damage was done to the works. Two of the leaders of the four sections taking part were among the missing. Squadron-Leader J. D. Nettleton, leader of another section, was awarded the Victoria Cross. This vivid impression of the raid, specially drawn for this book by Paul Nash, shows the "Lancasters," with enemy fighters in pursuit, accurately bombing their objective.

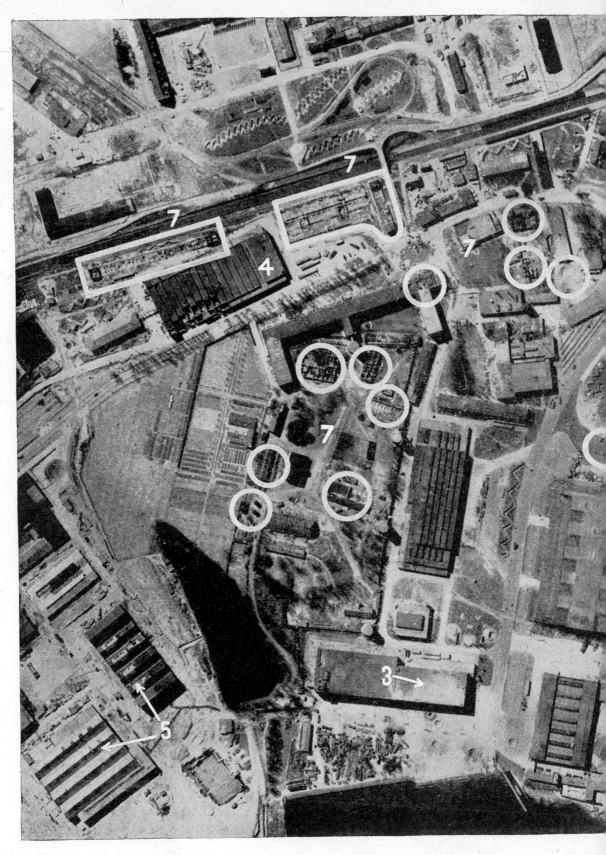

ROSTOCK BOMBED FOUR TIMES

23 TO 26 APRIL, 1942

On the night of 22-23 April the first of a series of four extremely heavy raids was carried out by the R.A.F. against the Baltic seaport town of Rostock. Like Luebeck, Rostock was an important port for the supply of Hitler's armies in Russia; it was also the site of the great Heinkel aircraft works and the Neptune shipbuilding yards engaged in the manufacture of U-boats and small craft for the German Navy. In the words of the Air Ministry communique, "an overmastering concentration" of "Stirlings," "Lancasters," "Manchesters," "Whitleys," "Wellingtons" and "Hampdens" was employed, and many fires were started in the Heinkel and Neptune works, and in the harbour area. The following night the raid was repeated, and crews reported that great fires, started in the first raid, were still raging in the town. Two more raids on the 25th and 26th added to the considerable damage already done, and aerial photographs taken by reconnaissance aircraft showed that the population was leaving the town by the thousand in order to escape from the British bombs. The weight of bombs dropped in the four raids amounted to almost 800 tons. The picture reproduced here shows the Heinkel works after the raids. Numbers indicate: (1), Damage to the main assembly shop after a direct hit by a stick of bombs, note roof damage and the area (1A) damaged by blast; (2), fuselages, aircraft parts and aircraft salvaged from the shop; (3), assembly shop damaged by blast; (4), machine shop damaged by fire; (5) large workshops damaged by blast; (6), paint shop damaged by blast; (7) other buildings considerably damaged by fire and high explosive bombs.

GERMAN ARMY AVOIDS ANNIHILATION.   On 24 April the Germans succeeded in relieving their Sixteenth Army which had been encircled near Staraya Russa in February. During the two months it had been cut off, it had been kept supplied by air, and although its numbers had been seriously depleted, it had nevertheless remained intact as a fighting unit. The picture shows German soldiers surrendering to the Russians during the fighting in this region. The dead bodies of their comrades in the foreground bear witness to the doggedness of their resistance, and to their confidence in the promise, made by the German High Command, that they would be relieved.

FIRST OF THE BAEDEKER RAIDS. On 24 April the Luftwaffe raided the historic city of Exeter where considerable damage was inflicted on many ancient buildings and churches, including the famous cathedral, dating from 1107. This raid was followed by raids on Norwich, Bath and York, and an official spokesman in Berlin described them as reprisals for the damage done by the Royal Air Force to ancient buildings in the Baltic ports of Luebeck and Rostock and added that the Luftwaffe would "go all out to bomb every building in Britain marked with three stars in Baedeker." Above, the cathedral is seen standing amidst the ruins of Exeter the morning after the raid.

(1) Firemen outside St. Martin's Church, York, which was destroyed; (2) Damage in the residential quarter of Norwich; and (3) a hospital which has received a direct hit; (4) The interior of the burnt-out Guildhall, York; (5) Damaged houses in the centre

BOMBING OF THE CATHEDRAL CITIES. The Exeter raid was quickly followed by attacks on Bath (25th and 26th), Norwich (27th and 29th), and York (28th), in all of which buildings and monuments of great historic value were blasted or demolished. By choosing

of Bath; and (6) the remains of the Regina Hotel and the Assembly Hall; (7) Interior of Exeter Cathedral, where a bomb fell on the choir aisle and demolished St. James's Chapel and the Sacristy, as well as many priceless medieval stained-glass windows.

these undefended cities as its targets, the Luftwaffe as good as admitted that it was unable to reply on anything like the same scale to the R.A.F.s raids on military objectives in Germany, and was forced to seek targets in lightly protected areas where its losses would be small.

BURMA ROAD CUT. On 19 April a Japanese force estimated at five divisions (about 100,000 men), with strong tank and aerial support, began a new thrust northwards through the Shan states towards Lashio, the western terminus of the vital Burma Road along which China was supplied with munitions of war by the Allies. In spite of desperate Chinese resistance the enemy reached Kehsi Mansam, only seventy miles south of Lashio, on the 28th, and on the following day, after a lightning advance of seventy miles, they captured Lashio itself after a mass

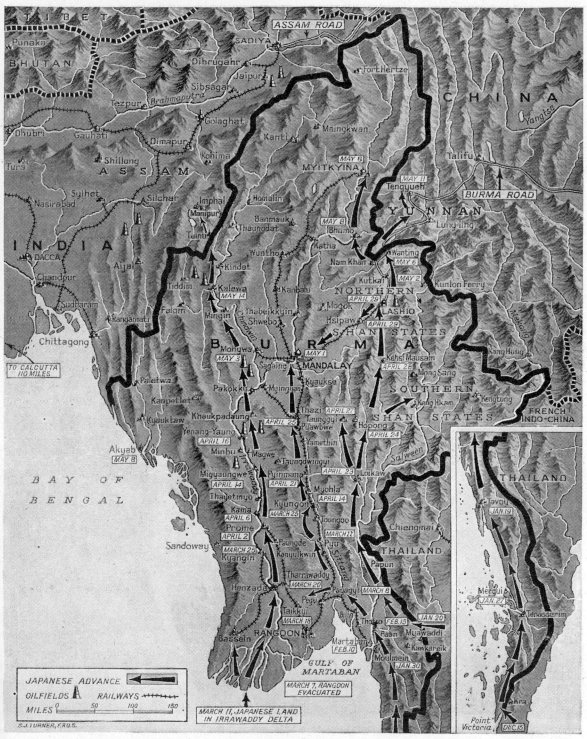

attack which was covered by a violent artillery and aerial barrage. On the same day the enemy captured Hsipaw, forty miles south-west of Lashio, thereby seriously threatening the rear of the Anglo-Chinese forces and, at the same time, cutting the railway to Mandalay. The pictures show: above, left, petrol lorries, carrying fuel for the Chinese air force during a halt on the Burma Road; below, left, supply vehicles negotiating some of the hairpin bends for which the road is famous. The map, drawn by S. J. Turner, shows the course of the campaign in Burma.

MANDALAY IN RUINS. After cutting the Lashio-Mandalay railway, the Japanese pressed rapidly on to Mandalay, which they occupied on 1 May. The beautiful city, with its many temples and pagodas, had been almost completely destroyed by enemy bombs, and the victorious army found only a shattered ruin with all roads, bridges and military installations wrecked. The British forces were withdrawn north of the Irrawaddy, and the famous Ava Bridge across the river was blown up. The pictures show: above, damage wrought by enemy bombs in Mandalay, and below, Japanese troops marching in triumph through a captured town during their advance.

Corregidor gives up the fight

JAPANESE LAND ON CORREGIDOR. Ever since the fall of Batan, on 9 April, the island fortress of Corregidor had been subjected to intense artillery fire at point-blank range from Japanese batteries on the mainland. This, together with heavy aerial bombardment, inflicted heavy casualties on the defenders as well as serious damage to military installations. On 5 May, after a particularly severe bombardment which swept away the beach defences, Japanese troops crossed the narrow channel separating Corregidor from the mainland and landed on the island. By the 6th the battle was over, and the gallant defenders, outnumbered and exhausted by lack of sleep, were forced to surrender. Altogether 11,574 prisoners were taken. General MacArthur (right), who planned the defence of the Philippines, had been in command there until he left in March to take over command in the South-west Pacific. His successor, General Wainwright, surrendered with his men. A general view of the island is given below.

THREAT TO MADAGASCAR REMOVED. With the object of forestalling a Japanese move against the French island of Madagascar, which would have given the enemy a valuable base for naval and air operations against the Allies in the Indian Ocean, a combined naval and military force made a landing at Courier Bay, on the western side of the island on 5 May, covered by naval aircraft. The main objective was the important naval base of Diego Suarez on the northern tip of the island, and after a British ultimatum for unconditional surrender had been rejected by the governor, the assault was begun. It consisted of a frontal thrust from the sea by warships

and aircraft, and an overland attack by the force that had landed at Courier Bay. The British troops soon gained control of the Andrakaka isthmus, thus cutting the naval base off from the rest of the island. The picture, specially drawn for this book by M. MacKinlay, shows British troops in landing barges, supported by aircraft of the Naval Air Arm, landing from transports in Courier Bay. Naval units, including an aircraft carrier, are standing offshore, ready if necessary to give support to the landing force. According to Vichy, light tanks were also landed and twelve British warships covered the landing. Little opposition was encountered at this stage of the operations.

BRITISH OVERCOME
The attack on Diego Suarez resolved itself into two main drives, one towards Diego Suarez itself, and the other towards Antsirana, on the south side of the bay. By the night of 5 May British forces had occupied Diego Suarez but on the 6th the southern attack was repulsed by French troops. Later in the day, however, after a fresh assault, British troops penetrated the town and forced the defenders to surrender. This attack was assisted by a diversion by fifty Royal Marines who were landed from a destroyer in Antsirana after a bold dash past the coastal defences. On the morning of the 7th, the coastal

FRENCH RESISTANCE
batteries on the Orangea
promontory, to the east of
Anisrana, were silenced
and with this all resistance
in the north of the island
came to an end. The
pictures show: above,
left, an invasion barge
ferrying a motor ambu-
lance to the shore during
the landing operations,
and right, the British
Commanders, Rear-
Admiral Syfret and Major-
General Sturges, inspect-
ing British troops after
the surrender. A German
ship which its crew had
unsuccessfully tried to
scuttle is seen, below,
left, in Diego Suarez harbour, and on the right
are French Colonial
troops who defended
the island, and later
joined the Free French.

BATTLE OF THE CORAL SEA

4-8 MAY, 1942.

Early in March, aerial reconnaissance showed that the Japanese were concentrating large numbers of transports and warships at Salamaua and Lae with the object of attacking Port Moresby and, eventually Australia. On 10 March, U.S. and Australian aircraft heavily attacked these forces and inflicted such damage that the enemy invasion plans had to be postponed. In April, however, the enemy began to regroup his forces, and early in May he seized bases in the Solomon and Louisiade Islands. On the 4th a task force of the U.S. Pacific Fleet found part of the Japanese invasion fleet at Tulagi (Solomons), and almost annihilated it, and three days later U.S. ships struck at the main body of the Japanese Fleet in the Coral Sea. In the action that followed, the first naval battle in history in which all the damage was done by aircraft, the enemy aircraft carrier "Ryukaku" and a heavy cruiser were sunk. The pictures show how, attacked by bomb and torpedo, the "Ryukaku" met her doom. She was turning into wind to launch her own aircraft when she was hit. On the right she is seen as the first bombs struck home; below, left, she is burning furiously whilst U.S. naval aircraft (in circles) manœuvre for a fresh attack. On the right her flight deck is almost awash as she settles down. A few minutes later she blew up and sank.

LOSS OF THE "LEXINGTON." On 8 May, whilst U.S. aircraft were still attacking the Japanese Fleet, the enemy launched a counter-attack and scored several hits with bombs and torpedoes on the 33,000-ton U.S. aircraft carrier, "Lexington." Several hours after the battle, while steaming at 20 knots, the "Lexington" was rocked by a terrific internal explosion, probably caused by the ignition of petrol vapours from leaks in the ruptured petrol lines. As the flames grew, and the "Lexington" was stopped, all its machinery disabled, the captain ordered the crew to abandon ship. Ninety-two per cent of the ship's company were rescued and reached port safely. The last man on the ship was the commanding officer, Captain Sherman, and as he slid down a line into the water, a

torpedo in the warhead locker exploded, and the "Lexington" sank soon afterwards. The picture shows the crew abandoning ship shortly after the explosion. A U.S. destroyer, which had come alongside to render assistance, can be seen through the smoke which envelops the carrier's superstructure. The U.S. attacks on Salamaua and Lae, and the Battle of the Coral Sea, besides foiling the enemy's invasion plans, cost him the aircraft carrier "Ryukaku," three heavy cruisers, one light cruiser, two destroyers, and several transports sunk, a cruiser and a destroyer probably sunk, and damage to a second aircraft carrier, the "Syokaku," which was hit on 8 May, and left ablaze. American losses were the "Lexington," the destroyer "Sims," and the 25,000-ton tanker "Neosho."

Russian winter advance

RUSSIAN COUNTER ATTACKS. After the failure of the German attempt to capture Moscow, the Russian armies took the offensive all along the front and drove the enemy back over a large part of the ground he had overrun. The Germans, however, succeeded in holding most of the important railheads and in clinging to their positions around Leningrad which, despite furious attacks, the Russians failed to relieve. The map, specially drawn by S. J. Turner, F.R.G.S., shows the territory (shaded dark) recaptured during the Russian winter offensive.

START OF GERMAN SPRING OFFENSIVE. On 8 May, German and Rumanian forces, under General von Manstein, launched a limited local offensive in the Crimea with the object of clearing that area of Russian troops and safeguarding their right flank against any possible Russian attack. In face of very strong pressure the Soviet forces slowly withdrew, inflicting heavy casualties on the enemy as they retreated. On the 15th, the enemy penetrated the suburbs of Kerch, and on the following day they claimed to have captured the town. The pictures show: above, Russian tanks, followed by infantry, advancing through enemy shell fire during a counter-attack in the Crimea; and below, Russian troops, using their tanks as cover, firing at the advancing Germans.

RUSSIAN ARMIES STRIKE FIRST. In order to forestall a probable German attack, Marshal Timoshenko on 13 May, launched an offensive on a fifty-mile front stretching from Chuguyev to Volchansk and quickly made deep penetrations into German defensive positions covering Kharkov. By the 15th, Russian forces had crossed the Donets and had advanced ten miles west of the river. On the 17th, in an effort to envelop Kharkov from north and south, the Russians broadened their front, which now stretched for 100 miles from Byelgorod to Smiyev, and

particularly heavy tank battles raged around the latter place, where giant Russian and American tanks scored notable successes against the enemy. Between 12 and 16 May, Soviet forces liberated 300 inhabited localities in advances varying from twelve to thirty-eight miles, besides killing about 12,000 enemy troops. The pictures show: loft, German machine gunners in action against the advancing Russians, and right, a German sentry outside a factory on the outskirts of Kharkov that has been set on fire by Russian artillery bombarding the town.

GERMAN COUNTER-OFFENSIVE. In order to hold up the Russian drive towards Kharkov, von Bock, on 19 May, launched a strong counter-offensive in the Izyum-Barenkovo area where he struck hard at the Donets River crossings. As a result he succeeded in halting the Russian push farther north, and on the 29th, Berlin announced that the Kharkov battle had ended with Kharkov still in German hands. Meanwhile, on the 23rd, the Russians had been obliged to evacuate the Kerch Peninsula and the German right flank was now secure against attack from the rear. The pictures show: above, a street in a Russian village destroyed by the advancing Germans, and below, German tank and motor cycle reinforcements rushing up to the front line to take part in their new drive.

M. MOLOTOV IN LONDON. On 21 May, M. Molotov arrived in London to put his signature to a twenty-year treaty of alliance between Great Britain and the Soviet Union. The signatories undertook to give each other military and other assistance against the Axis and agreed not to conclude a separate peace with the enemy. They also agreed to collaborate with one another and with the other United Nations in the peace settlement and during the ensuing period of reconstruction on the basis of the principles set out in the Atlantic Charter. The picture above shows, Mr. Eden, watched by the Prime Minister, putting his signature to the treaty; on his right are M. Molotov and M. Maisky. The powerful Russian bomber that brought M. Molotov to Britain is seen below.

GERMAN OFFENSIVE IN LIBYA
26 MAY, 1942

After heavy dive bombing attacks on the British positions in Libya, General Rommel, on 26 May, launched a full scale offensive with the object of defeating the British armoured forces and capturing Tobruk. His plan of campaign was to capture Bir Hakeim, at the southern end of the British mine-field and send the Afrika Korps, supported by German and Italian mobile divisions, round the southern end of the minefields. At the same time a holding attack was to be made on the British positions running south from Gazala to the Trigh Capuzzo. On the night of 26-27 May, Rommel carried out the first part of his plan, the Afrika Korps passing round Bir Hakeim and advancing rapidly towards Acroma and towards El Duda and Sidi Rezegh, which some of his forward troops actually reached before being driven back by British armoured columns. A few enemy tanks reached the escarpment overlooking the coastal road north of Acroma, but were driven back. On the same night the enemy attempted a landing from the sea at this spot with the object of joining up with the tanks, but this was frustrated by naval forces working in close co-operation with the army. Before the Axis forces reached El Adem or Acroma, they were brought to action by British armoured divisions and turned back. The attack on the British positions between Gazala and Trigh Capuzzo, made on the 27th, was repulsed with heavy casualties and an attack on Bir Hakeim by the Italian Mobile Corps was repulsed by the Free French. The pictures, taken during the opening stages of the offensive, show: above, part of a German armoured division advancing through a heavy artillery barrage put up by British batteries, and below, Axis tanks being rushed up to the main battle area to reinforce their hard-pressed armoured forces.

ENEMY ATTACK REPULSED. After their failure to reach Tobruk, the German tank formations which had been advancing in two columns towards El Adem and Acroma, reunited in the neighbourhood of Knightsbridge, twelve miles south of Acroma, where they were engaged by British armoured forces and heavy fighting developed. This continued until the 30th, the battle swaying backwards and forwards over a wide area from Acroma in the north to Bir Hakeim, and from El Adem to the British minefields.   By the 30th the enemy, finding himself running short of supplies and water, forced two gaps in the British minefields and attempted to pass his forces through these.   By the morning of 1 June he had succeeded in withdrawing many of his vehicles and was bringing up guns

to cover their retreat.   A large number of his tanks, however, and many transport vehicles remained to the east of the minefield, and these were ceaselessly attacked by British troops and the R.A.F., and many of them were destroyed.   It was estimated that during this period at least 600 enemy vehicles were put out of action, and in Cairo it was authoritatively stated that the Afrika Korps had taken a severe knock and that the position remained "not unfavourable" to the British.   The pictures show: left, above, a mobile British anti-tank gun passing a knocked-out German tank, and below, British soldiers examining the damage done to a German tank by the accurate fire of British guns.   On the right, a South African patrol is seen sheltering from enemy mortar fire.

BIGGEST AIR RAID IN HISTORY. On the night of 30 May, a force of more than 1,000 bombers attacked the Ruhr and Rhineland, with Cologne as the main objective. The attack was concentrated into the space of one and a half hours and more than 2,000 tons of bombs were dropped. Cologne, the fourth largest city of the Reich, was an important centre of rail communications for the whole of Western Germany and the seat of many vital war industries. The weight of the attack soon overwhelmed the ground defences, and pilots who took

part described it as "too gigantic to be real."   Air reconnaissance on the following day reported that the fires of Cologne were visible from the Dutch coast and that a great pall of smoke, rising to 15,000 feet, enveloped the city.   Forty-four, less than five per cent, of the attacking force were lost.   The picture, specially drawn by Charles Cundall, A.R.A., shows the centre of the city during the height of the attack.   The fact that the famous Cathedral (in foreground) was untouched was a striking tribute to the accuracy of the British bombing.

RAID DAMAGE IN COLOGNE. The raid on Cologne was officially described as an "outstanding success," and photographs obtained by reconnaissance aircraft showed extensive damage in the city, particularly in the industrial area. It was estimated that at least 250 factory buildings and workshops were destroyed, or severely damaged. The Cologne raid was followed by a 1,000-bomber attack on Essen on 1 June. The pictures show the workshops of the Koelnischer Gummifaden Fabrik, at Deutz, a suburb of Cologne, on the east bank of the Rhine, before and after the raid. This factory was engaged in the manufacture of tyres and inner tubes for German army lorries.

REPRISAL FOR COLOGNE RAID. On the last night of May, a small force of enemy bombers raided Canterbury, where considerable damage was caused in the shopping centre and many people were rendered homeless. The German High Command described the raid as a "reprisal for the terrorist raid on Cologne," and Berlin radio said that Canterbury, "a main centre of English hypocrisy," had to pay for the attack on the old beautiful city on the Rhine. Although no bombs hit the Cathedral, several fell nearby, causing damage by blast. The picture shows Dr. Hewlett Johnson, Dean of Canterbury, inspecting the damaged Cathedral library.

BATTLE OF MIDWAY ISLAND
3-7 JUNE, 1942

On 3 June, two large Japanese fleets, one composed mainly of transports, and the other of battleships, aircraft carriers, cruisers and destroyers, approached Midway Island, the U.S. naval and air base in the Pacific. Their object was to capture the island and gain for themselves yet another base for operations against the Allies. As soon as the enemy's presence was reported a strong force of U.S. Army bombers set out to locate the Japanese fleet, and in the attack that followed direct hits were scored on eight enemy ships. Meanwhile a force of about 180 Japanese aircraft from aircraft carriers raided the airfields, docks and harbour installations on the island, but succeeded in inflicting only minor damage. The strength of the U.S. attack, and the arrival of powerful units of the American Pacific Fleet, forced the Japanese to withdraw, and during the four following days the enemy were subjected to almost non-stop attacks with bomb and torpedo and tremendous casualties were inflicted on his ships. The losses, the greatest sustained by the enemy since war began, amounted to four aircraft carriers, two of 26,900 tons and two of 10,000 tons sunk; two battleships damaged, one severely, two heavy cruisers of the Mogami class sunk and three damaged, one light cruiser damaged and three destroyers sunk. In addition, four transports were hit by bombs and torpedoes; and one, and probably two, were sunk. U.S. losses amounted to one aircraft carrier, the "Yorktown," and the destroyer "Hamman."

The pictures show: above, the U.S. aircraft carrier "Yorktown" (left) and a cruiser throwing up an umbrella of A.A. fire to beat off a squadron of Japanese torpedo bombers attacking the carrier during the battle. At the waterline level, extreme left, a column of smoke shows where an enemy plane has been shot down. On the left is a Japanese 8,500-ton cruiser of the Mogami class after it has been hit by U.S. bombs and left in a sinking condition. Japanese seamen can be seen crowded together on the stern of the battered and blazing warship before abandoning it.

PEARL HARBOUR AVENGED. It was estimated that the Japanese lost 275 aircraft and 6,000 men in the four aircraft carriers sunk in the Battle of Midway Island, and that their total losses amounted to 18,000 men. The carriers "Kaga" and "Akagi," both ships of 26,900 tons, were the largest ships of their type in the Japanese Navy.

The other carriers sunk were the 10,000-ton "Hiryu" and "Soryu," each of which carried between thirty and forty aircraft. The picture, specially drawn by Arthur J. W. Burgess, R.I., R.B.S., shows the "Kaga" class ships, with their escorts of battleships and destroyers, under heavy attack from U.S. bomb- and torpedo-carrying planes.

BATTLE OF THE MINEFIELDS Whilst the enemy was endeavouring to withdraw his forces through the gaps he had made in the British minefields, British mobile forces harassed his supply lines from the west and on 1 June, captured the strong point of Rotunda Segnali, thirty miles west of the main British positions. Meanwhile considerable fighting continued in the area west of Knightsbridge and around Bir Hakeim, where Free French forces under General Koenig were clinging desperately to this vital bastion of the British line. On 4 June British armoured forces drove the enemy out o Tamar, six miles west of Knightsbridge, and on the following day, British and Indian troops with American-built " General Grant " tanks in support, launched a spirited counter-attack against Rommel's panzer forces in the "Devil's Cauldron" (west of Knightsbridge) and around the gaps in the minefields, through which the enemy was now bringing supplies and reinforcements. On the 6th a strong enemy attack 'n this area was successfully repulsed and the German Twenty-First Panzer Division was driven out of Harmat. Three days later, after having rejected five Axis ultimatums to surrender, the Free French at Bir Hakeim, aided by British armoured and motorized forces, beat off the heaviest enemy attack yet launched on this sector, but on the following day, owing to the increasing difficulty in getting supplies through to the garrison, the Free French were withdrawn after having stood up to incessant dive bombing and artillery bombardment for sixteen days. The maps show : above the stages of the German advance in Libya prior to the opening of the offensive on 26 May, and below the progress of the fighting during the first six days. The picture above shows British tanks moving up to the main battle line near Knightsbridge.

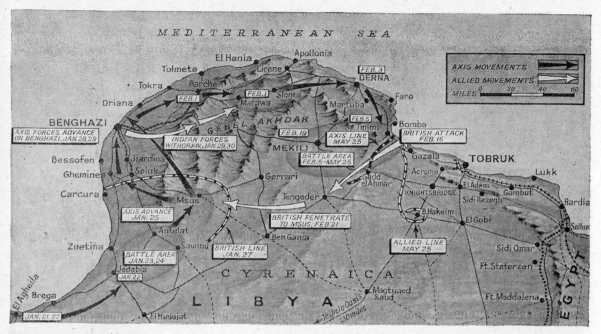

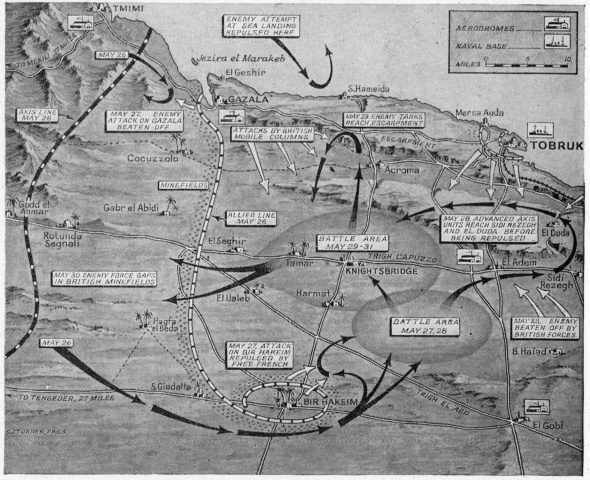

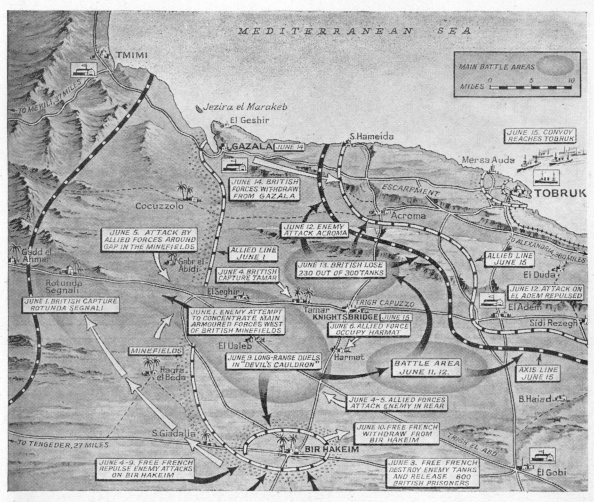

MEDITERRANEAN SEA

MAIN BATTLE AREAS

MILES 0 5 10

TMIMI

TO MEKILI, 37 MILES

Jezira el Marakeb
El Geshir

S.Hameida

GAZALA JUNE 14

JUNE 15. CONVOY REACHES TOBRUK

Mersa Auda

ESCARPMENT

TOBRUK

JUNE 14. BRITISH FORCES WITHDRAW FROM GAZALA

Cocuzzolo

Acroma

JUNE 12. ENEMY ATTACK ACROMA

TO ALEXANDRIA, 380 MILES

JUNE 5. ATTACK BY ALLIED FORCES AROUND GAP IN THE MINEFIELDS

ALLIED LINE JUNE 1

ALLIED LINE JUNE 15

Gadd el Ahmar

Gabr el Abidi

JUNE 4 BRITISH CAPTURE TAMAR

JUNE 13. BRITISH LOSE 230 OUT OF 300 TANKS

El Duda

Rotunda Segnali

El Seghir

Tamar

TRIGH CAPUZZO

JUNE 12. ATTACK ON EL ADEM REPULSED

JUNE 1. BRITISH CAPTURE ROTUNDA SEGNALI

JUNE 1. ENEMY ATTEMPT TO CONCENTRATE MAIN ARMOURED FORCES WEST OF BRITISH MINEFIELDS

KNIGHTSBRIDGE JUNE 15

El Adem

Sidi Rezegh

JUNE 6. ALLIED FORCE OCCUPY HARMAT

MINEFIELDS

El Ualeb

JUNE 9. LONG-RANGE DUELS IN "DEVIL'S CAULDRON"

Harmat

BATTLE AREA JUNE 11, 12.

AXIS LINE JUNE 15

Hagfa el Beda

B.Haiad

JUNE 4-5. ALLIED FORCES ATTACK ENEMY IN REAR

S.Giadalla

TO TENGEDER, 27 MILES

BIR HAKEIM

JUNE 10. FREE FRENCH WITHDRAW FROM BIR HAKEIM

TRIGH EL ABD

JUNE 4-9. FREE FRENCH REPULSE ENEMY ATTACKS ON BIR HAKEIM

JUNE 3. FREE FRENCH DESTROY ENEMY TANKS AND RELEASE 600 BRITISH PRISONERS

El Gobi

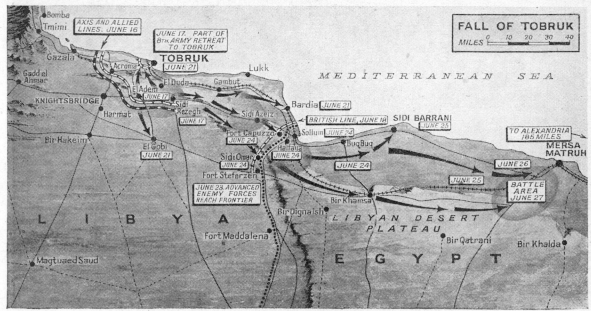

Bomba
Tmimi

AXIS AND ALLIED LINES, JUNE 16

JUNE 17. PART OF 8TH.ARMY RETREAT TO TOBRUK

Gazala

TOBRUK JUNE 21

Lukk

FALL OF TOBRUK

MILES 0 10 20 30 40

Gadd el Ahmar

Acroma

El Duda

Gambut

MEDITERRANEAN SEA

KNIGHTSBRIDGE

El Adem JUNE 17

Sidi Rezegh JUNE 17

Sidi Azeiz

Bardia JUNE 21

SIDI BARRANI JUNE 25

Harmat

BRITISH LINE, JUNE 18

Bir Hakeim

El Gobi JUNE 21

Fort Capuzzo JUNE 24

Sollum JUNE 24

TO ALEXANDRIA 185 MILES

MERSA MATRUH

Sidi Omar JUNE 24

Halfaya JUNE 24

BuqBuq

JUNE 26

Fort Sterferzen

JUNE 24

JUNE 25

BATTLE AREA JUNE 27

JUNE 23. ADVANCED ENEMY FORCES REACH FRONTIER

Bir Dignaish

Bir Khamsa

LIBYAN DESERT PLATEAU

L I B Y A

Fort Maddalena

Bir Qatrani

Bir Khalda

E G Y P T

Magtua ed Saud

BLACK DAY FOR THE EIGHTH ARMY. Within a few hours of the withdrawal from Bir Hakeim a new tank battle flared up in the area east of Harmat where the enemy made a strong thrust towards El Adem. This was repulsed on the 12th and the Axis armoured forces swung round in a wide arc and attacked Acroma, where they were heavily engaged by British tanks and aircraft. The turning point in the battle was reached on the 13th. In the afternoon of that day strong British armoured formations attempting to break up Axis tank concentrations ran into concealed anti-tank batteries near Bir Behaffar, on the Trigh Capuzzo, and suffered very severe losses which completely changed the course of the battle. In the morning the British had 300 tanks in the field—by nightfall only seventy remained. This disaster necessitated the withdrawal of British troops from the Knightsbridge area and also of the South African Division from Gazala. The next enemy move was a strong thrust in the direction of El Adem. This was stubbornly resisted by the remnants of the British armoured forces, but after four days' fierce fighting General Ritchie, on 17 June, decided to withdraw his forces to the El Adem-Sidi Rezegh-El Duda area and to concentrate his main strength on the Egyptian frontier. At the same time he left what he considered to be a sufficiently strong force to hold Tobruk. The map, above, left, shows the course of the fighting between 1 and 15 June. The lower map shows the retreat of the Eighth Army into Egypt, carried out between 16 and 27 June, and described fully on later pages. The picture shows an Axis armoured attack in full progress during the fierce fighting for Bir Hakeim. The clash of tanks is seen in the distance, whilst dive bombers operate overhead.

NEW GERMAN ATTACKS IN RUSSIA. The fighting in the Kharkov sector died down towards the end of May and there was a period of comparative quiet which lasted until 10 June when a fresh German attack was launched to recapture the strong points in their defences round Kharkov taken by Marshal Timoshenko in his recent offensive. On the 25th the Russians evacuated Kupiansk, an important rail junction sixty miles south-east of Kharkov, and on the following day they had to abandon Izyum, on the Donets, the scene of the great tank battles a month earlier. The pictures show: above, Nazi tanks passing a burning church during their advance, and below, Soviet infantry riding into battle on the backs of their tanks during a counter-attack.

Japanese land on Aleutian Islands

JAPANESE LAND AT KISKA. On 13 June, the U.S. Navy Department announced that Japanese landings had taken place at Attu and Kiska, in the Aleutian Islands, 1,300 miles from the Alaskan mainland and only 600 miles from the new American naval base at Dutch Harbour. Bad weather prevented immediate action, but on the 15th, U.S. forces attacked the enemy and sank one cruiser and severely damaged three other cruisers, an aircraft carrier, a destroyer and a gunboat. A few days later a number of transports were observed at anchor in Kiska harbour and were attacked by U.S. Army bombers, which succeeded in sinking one. The picture shows the ship ablaze shortly before she sank. Two other transports can be seen on the left and right of the picture.

GERMANS CAPTURE TOBRUK
AND MERSA MATRUH
18-29 JUNE, 1942

After the withdrawal of the British forces to the Egyptian frontier, mobile formations harassed enemy columns pushing eastwards towards Bardia and turned them back about twenty-five miles from the town. On the 20th, however, Rommel's tank forces suddenly switched their attack towards Tobruk from the direction of El Adem and El Duda and succeeded, with the help of massed dive bomber attacks, in forcing a gap on a narrow front in the south-east perimeter defences through which tanks and lorried infantry passed. On the 21st, after desperate fighting, the town and port were occupied and the garrison of 25,000 was forced to surrender. On the same day the enemy occupied Bardia. By the 26th, after capturing Capuzzo, Sollum, Helafaya and Sidi Barrani, the enemy had got within fifteen miles of Mersa Matruh, and on the next day battle was joined with his main armoured forces. As a result Mersa Matruh fell on the 29th and the British and Imperial forces fell back in good order whilst mobile columns, assisted by the R.A.F., the S.A.A.F. and the U.S. Army Air Corps, slowed down the enemy advance. The pictures show: left, Italian infantry taking up positions prior to the Axis attack on Tobruk; left, below, some of the Imperial troops taken prisoner in Tobruk; and right, British gunners in action before Mersa Matruh.

GERMANY'S GIANT PINCER MOVEMENT. Germany's simultaneous offensives in Southern Russia and in Egypt were not isolated military campaigns, but closely connected parts of a vast strategic whole. Just as the Murmansk and Leningrad fronts together formed the left wing of the attack upon Russia, so the combined Ukrainian and African fronts formed the right wing. Within this right wing, the enemy was hoping to develop a vast pincer movement. The southern arm, through Egypt and Syria, stretched out towards the oilfields of Irak and Iran and the key river-port of Basra; the northern arm, from Rostov and Kharkov, aimed at the Caucasian

222

oilfields which supplied most of Russia's needs. If these two arms ever met, Germany would gain much more than oil. The Mediterranean would become a German lake, the southern supply route to Russia via the Persian Gulf would be severed, the British Empire would be cut in half and the wealth of Africa, India and the East would be exposed to enemy exploitation. In the path of the enemy stood the armies of Timoshenko at Rostov and of Auchinleck at Alexandria. It was to these forces that the Allies looked to frustrate this great strategic aim. This map, specially drawn by S. J. Turner, shows at a glance this grandiose Axis plan.

223

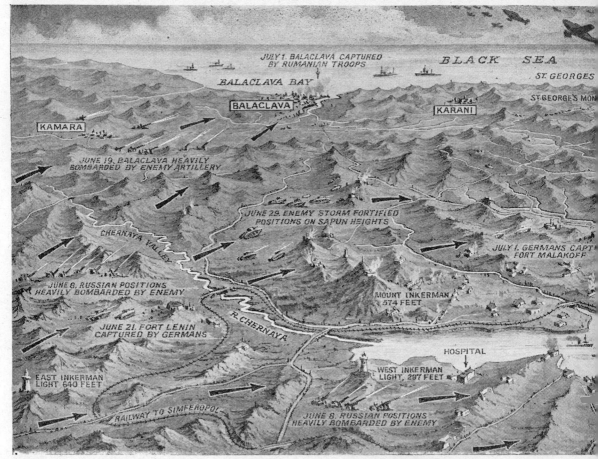

JULY 1. BALACLAVA CAPTURED BY RUMANIAN TROOPS

BLACK SEA

ST. GEORGES

BALACLAVA BAY

ST. GEORGE'S MON

BALACLAVA

KARANI

KAMARA

JUNE 19. BALACLAVA HEAVILY BOMBARDED BY ENEMY ARTILLERY

JUNE 29. ENEMY STORM FORTIFIED POSITIONS ON SAPUN HEIGHTS

JULY 1. GERMANS CAPT FORT MALAKOFF

CHERNAYA VALLEY

JUNE 8. RUSSIAN POSITIONS HEAVILY BOMBARDED BY ENEMY

MOUNT INKERMAN 574 FEET

JUNE 21. FORT LENIN CAPTURED BY GERMANS

R. CHERNAYA

HOSPITAL

EAST INKERMAN LIGHT 640 FEET

WEST INKERMAN LIGHT, 297 FEET

RAILWAY TO SIMFEROPOL

JUNE 8. RUSSIAN POSITIONS HEAVILY BOMBARDED BY ENEMY

FALL OF

On 4 June the German forces, who had been investing Sevastopol since the previous November, launched a big attack on the naval base. Into this attack they threw 100,000 men and hundreds of tanks and dive bombers, and employed heavy siege artillery on a vast scale. By these tactics they hoped to blast their way into the defences by sheer weight of metal. By the 14th they had captured Fort Stalin after bitter hand-to-hand fighting, and by the 20th they had occupied most of the Russian positions north of Severnaya Bay. Still the defenders refused to admit defeat; still they continued to inflict enormous casualties on the attackers,

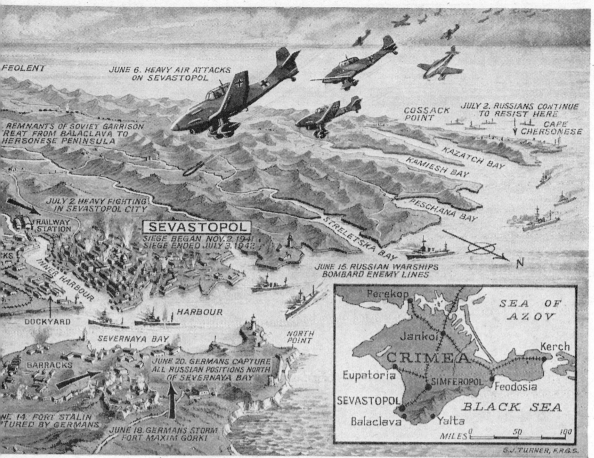

FEOLENT

JUNE 6. HEAVY AIR ATTACKS ON SEVASTOPOL

COSSACK POINT

JULY 2. RUSSIANS CONTINUE TO RESIST HERE

CAPE CHERSONESE

REMNANTS OF SOVIET GARRISON RETREAT FROM BALACLAVA TO HERSONESE PENINSULA

KAZATCH BAY

KAMIESH BAY

JULY 2. HEAVY FIGHTING IN SEVASTOPOL CITY

PESCHANA BAY

RAILWAY STATION

SEVASTOPOL
SIEGE BEGAN NOV. 2, 1941.
SIEGE ENDED JULY 3, 1942.

STRELETSKA BAY

JUNE 15. RUSSIAN WARSHIPS BOMBARD ENEMY LINES

INNER HARBOUR

DOCKYARD

HARBOUR

NORTH POINT

N

SEVERNAYA BAY

BARRACKS

JUNE 20. GERMANS CAPTURE ALL RUSSIAN POSITIONS NORTH OF SEVERNAYA BAY

JUNE 14. FORT STALIN CAPTURED BY GERMANS

JUNE 18. GERMANS STORM FORT MAXIM GORKI

Perekop

SEA OF AZOV

Jankoi

CRIMEA

Kerch

Eupatoria

SIMFEROPOL

Feodosia

SEVASTOPOL

BLACK SEA

Balaclava

Yalta

MILES 0   50   100

S. J. TURNER, F.R.G.S.

SEVASTOPOL

who were said to be advancing over mountains of their own dead. On 1 July Berlin claimed that the fortress, town and harbour were in their hands, that their infantry had stormed Malakoff Fort, and that Rumanian troops had taken Balaclava. But it was not until the 3rd that all resistance was finally overcome. The pictures show: left, bombs from enemy dive bombers bursting on Russian defensive positions; right, a German armoured vehicle passing through the battered remains of the town. The map, specially drawn by S. J. Turner, F.R.G.S., shows the fortress and surrounding territory together with the direction of German attacks.

A CITY IN RUINS. The fall of Sevastopol was a severe blow to the Russian cause. The great naval base, home of the Black Sea Fleet, was of the utmost strategic importance to the enemy, for not only did its capture remove the last remaining threat to his right flank, but it gave him a base from which he could in the future carry out landing operations south of the Caucasus Mountains. This would threaten the port of Batum and the vital oil centre of Baku. In addition its loss would seriously restrict the free movements of the Black Sea Fleet, which was now well within the

range of enemy bombers. The defence of Sevastopol forms one of the most glorious episodes in the annals of military history, and the picture shows how the defenders heroically c.ung on to their positions until the who.e town was reduced to a complete shambles. Those civilians who were not evacuated lived under unspeakable conditions, yet, together with the soldiers and the marines of the Black Sea Fleet, they defied the might of the German Army for many months and set a fine example to all the peoples of the world fighting in the cause of freedom.

DEFENCE OF VORONEZH. On 28 June the Germans began a new offensive in the Kursk sector, 120 miles north of Kharkov, the object of which was to capture the important rail junction of Voronezh, on the Moscow-Rostov railway, 130 miles east of Kharkov. This would have given the Germans a strong defensive bastion on the flank of their attack farther south. By early July, fighting on a tremendous scale had also developed in the Byelgorod and Volchansk areas (between Kursk and Kharkov), where thousands of tanks, closely followed by infantry and supported by masses of dive bombers, battered at the Russian positions. In face of tremendous pressure the Russian armies slowly withdrew in good order, taking terrible toll of the enemy as they retired. On 7 July the Germans succeeded in establishing bridgeheads on the east bank of the Don opposite Voronezh across which

they managed to throw an infantry division and 100 tanks. The crossings, however, were under continual fire from Russian artillery and aerial bombardment by Stormovik dive bombers, and the Russians launched repeated counter-attacks with strong forces of tanks and infantry. According to Russian reports the Don was flowing red with the blood of dead Germans. Meanwhile, farther south, the enemy was pushing eastwards in an attempt to gain control of the middle reaches of the Don. On the 8th the Russians evacuated Stary Oskol, and two days later they abandoned Rossosh after severe battles in which as many as 8,000 tanks were locked in combat on a front 110 miles long. The picture shows the ruins of a bridge across the Don blown up by the Russians. German troops can be seen threading their way past smashed lorries and cars, which litter the ground for miles around.

BATTLE OF

After the fall of Mersa Matruh, Rommel continued his advance eastwards, and by 1 July he had reached El Alamein, only sixty miles from Alexandria. It was here that General Auchinleck decided to make a stand, for the country formed a narrow bottleneck, the sea guarding his right flank, and the Qattara Depression his left. In the early morning of 1 July the armoured strength of the opposing forces joined battle, and heavy fighting continued throughout the day. The Eighth Army repulsed repeated attacks by tanks and lorried infantry, and on the evening of the 2nd the enemy retired, leaving the British positions intact. On the following day the British forces, with air support on a scale unprecedented on the Middle Eastern Front, counter-attacked, captured several hundred prisoners, and put many

EGYPT BEGINS

enemy tanks out of action. This was followed on the 10th by an attack by British and South African troops, with tank and air support, who occupied the ridge of Tel el Eisa, after an advance of five miles along the railway from El Alamein. Eighteen enemy tanks were destroyed, and more than 2 000 prisoners were taken in this operation. A similar attack was made from the south on the 15th by New Zealand and Indian infantry who succeeded in taking Ruweisat Ridge, south of El Alamein and advancing into the enemy positions, to a depth of seven miles. The pictures show: above, left, British tanks setting off at dawn to attack enemy positions, and right, Matildas, followed by men of the Scots Guards, going into action at El Alamein. The lower pictures show Bren carriers patrolling the forward areas of the battlefield.

FIGHTING IN THE DON BEND. Although the Germans had reached the very gates of Voronezh, they were unable to take it by storm. Farther south, however, a rapid advance along the railways brought about the fall of Kantemirovka (south of Rossosh) and of Lisichansk (100 miles south-west of Kantemirovka) on 12 July, and heavy fighting was in progress near Boguchar which, together with Millerovsk, the Russians were obliged to evacuate on the 15th. This created a dangerous bulge in the Russian lines which threatened the great industrial city of Stalingrad, on the Volga, and the port of Rostov at the mouth of the Don. The Russian armies inside the Don

bend fought fierce rearguard actions whilst retiring to their main defensive positions along the lower reaches of the river, but by the 16th fighting was taking place before Voroshilovgrad, and two days later the enemy was only seventy miles north-west of Rostov, and still advancing rapidly. On the following day Voroshilovgrad was evacuated by the Red Army in order to avoid encirclement. The pictures show: left, Russian sappers on the Voronezh sector crawling forward to clear a gap in a minefield for the passage of their tanks and infantry, and right, Soviet infantry equipped with automatic weapons, awaiting the enemy in a village in the southern sector.

GERMAN COUNTER-ATTACKS REPELLED. On 16 July German forces attempted to recapture the positions they had lost on Ruweisat Ridge, and a big tank battle developed in which twenty-five enemy tanks were destroyed. In the north, where enemy counter-attacks had regained part of the ground lost on Tel el Eisa, Imperial forces drove the enemy out of most of the lost positions. On the 21st General Auchinleck launched a general offensive all along the front, and fierce fighting raged throughout the night and the following day. In this action South

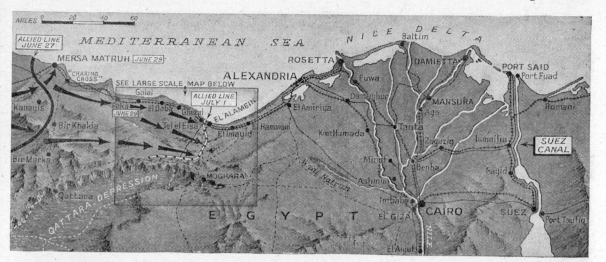

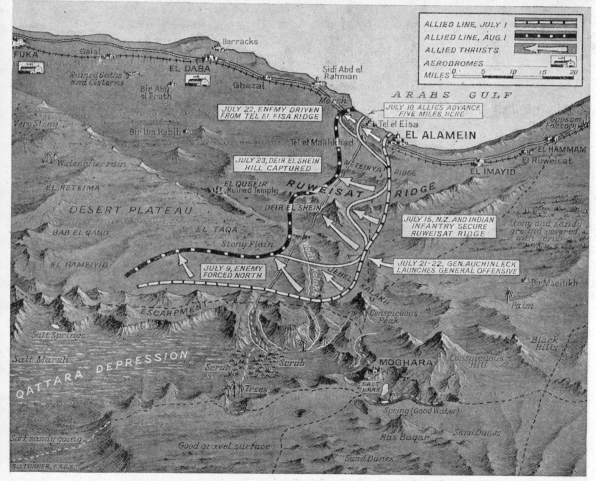

African troops drove the enemy from the whole of Tel el Eisa Ridge, whilst in the centre New Zealand infantry made considerable progress along Ruweisat Ridge. By the 25th fighting had died down, and the enemy began to "dig in." The pictures show: above, some of the Axis prisoners taken by the New Zealanders on Ruweisat Ridge, and below, loading up a General Grant tank ready for action. The maps show, above, the direction of the German advance from Mersa Matruh (indicated by black arrows), and below, the main battle area during July.

FIRE BOMBS FOR GERMAN CITIES. During July, Bomber Command kept up its attacks on centres of German war production whenever weather permitted. Bremen, Wilhelmshaven, Danzig, Flensburg, Dusseldorf, Duisburg, Luebeck, Vegesack and Hamburg were visited, some of them more than once, and great material damage was done. Of these raids perhaps the most outstanding were the daylight raid on Danzig on the 11th and the night raid on Hamburg on the 26th. The former involved a flight of 1,750 miles—the longest daylight

operational flight yet attempted. In the Hamburg raid 175,000 incendiary bombs were rained on the city within fifty minutes—far surpassing the number dropped on London in the fire raid of 29 December, 1940. Some idea of the weight of the British offensive may be gathered from the fact that during June and July, 1942, 13,000 tons of bombs were dropped on Germany as against 8,500 tons in the same months of 1941, and 3,500 in June and July, 1940. The "Stirling" bomber, seen above, is being loaded up with incendiary bombs in readiness for the raid.

FALL OF ROSTOV. After the evacuation of Voroshilovgrad, the German attack on Rostov was broadened by pressure both from Taganrog and Millerovo. On 25 July the enemy thrusts down the railways from Voroshilovgrad and Millerovo had linked up, and fighting on the whole Lower Don front became intense. Two bridges were thrown across the river at Tsymlyansk, and despite desperate Russian resistance, the railway joining Stalingrad with the Black Sea and the Caucasus was threatened. The superiority of the enemy in arms and numbers enabled him to consolidate his bridgehead and also to close in on Rostov. After carrying out

thorough demolitions, the great port was evacuated by the Russians on the 27th.   On the same day another enemy threat to the Black Sea coast and the oil of Maikop took shape in a swift German drive south-eastwards to Bataisk.   The pictures show: left, German infantry in Rostov crawling forward with the support of field guns; top, right, burnt-out tram cars which had been used as barricades by the Russians during the desperate street fighting which raged in the town and suburbs before the final evacuation.   The picture below, right, shows a party of German infantry surrendering to the crew of a Soviet tank during a Russian counter-attack.

RUSSIAN OILFIELDS THREATENED. After the German capture of Rostov and Bataisk, fierce and prolonged fighting took place near Salsk and at Kuschev. Again the Soviet forces were driven gradually back, and on 6 August von Kleist's tanks, after crossing the Kuban river, entered Tikhoretsk. The Germans were now advancing on Maikop across the rich Kuban steppes, and on the 8th, they broke through towards Armavir and Krasnodar, thereby developing a dangerous pincers threat to Maikop. The pictures show: left, above, Red Army men attacking an enemy outpost in an attempt to stem the advance, and below, German troops occupying a railway station that has been "scorched" by the retreating Russians. Right, above, Germans advancing along a road choked with refugees, whose homes have been destroyed; below, German riflemen attacking a building held by Russian troops.

U.S. MARINES LAND IN THE SOLOMONS

7 AUGUST, 1942

In the early hours of 7 August warships and aircraft of the U.S. Pacific Fleet opened up a heavy bombardment on the Japanese positions in the Tulagi area of the Solomons, and U.S. marines went ashore in landing barges. By nightfall they had gained strong positions on Guadalcanar, Tulagi, and Florida, after having overcome fierce enemy resistance, and on the following day they extended the occupied area of Guadalcanar and captured a vital aerodrome. On Tulagi almost all resistance had been overcome and huge quantities of munitions and supplies had been captured. By noon on the 10th the marines were in firm control of Guadalcanar, Tulagi, Gavatu, Tanambogo, Makambo and Florida, and were engaged in mopping up enemy forces who had retired into the interior. During these operations long-range U.S. bombers carried out extensive reconnaissance besides bombing enemy ships and air bases in New Britain, New Ireland, and in the Solomons area. The pictures show: left, U.S. marines landing on Guadalcanar, and below, left, unloading transport vehicles and supplies. Amphibious tanks that were used by the attackers are seen coming ashore, below right.

RIOTING IN INDIA. After the failure of Sir Stafford Cripps's mission to India, the Congress Party, on 10 July, issued a resolution demanding immediate British withdrawal. Shortly afterwards the Government of India raided Congress headquarters and seized the records of its proceedings. Amongst the documents confiscated was Gandhi's origina draft resolution, submitted to the Working Committee on 27 April, which contained a statement to the effect that if India were free one of her first steps would probably be to negotiate with Japan. The Government published the text of this draft on 4 August, and on the following day Congress passed an amended resolution restating its demand for British withdrawal and threatening a mass civil disobedience campaign if its demands were not met. As a result the Government, on the 7th, issued an order forbidding the closure of shops dealing with vital necessities, and on the 9th arrested 148 Congress leaders, including Gandhi, Pandit Nehru, and Dr. Azad. Rioting broke out in Bombay and other cities and the police and military were called out to deal with the disturbances. Altogether 658 people were killed and 1,003 wounded by police and military action. Government forces casualties amounted to thirty-one police and eleven military killed, and a large number injured. The pictures show: above, the Yervada Palace, Poona, where Gandhi was imprisoned, and below, a picture of Gandhi taken in London in 1931.

RUSSIAN OIL TOWN CAPTURED. After the German break through towards Armavir and Krasnodar, the defenders, on 9 August, set the oilfields on fire and demolished all equipment. The Germans made unsuccessful attempts to blast out the fires by dropping demolition charges from aircraft near the blazing wells. On the 16th the town of Maikop had to be abandoned. The enemy also made rapid progress towards the Black Sea port of Novorossisk and along the northern side of the main Caucasus range. On the 10th they captured Piatigorsk, 120 miles south-east of Armavir, and four days later they entered Georgievsk, 120 miles north-west of the Grozny oilfields, on the Rostov-Baku railway. Meanwhile, in the Don bend, the enemy continued to throw masses of men into the battle regardless of huge losses. On the 15th he succeeded in driving a wedge into the Russian positions at the Don elbow between Kletskaya and Kalach, forty miles north-west of Stalingrad, but in face of strong Soviet counter-attacks no enemy units succeeded in crossing the river. The pictures show: above, German troops captured by the Russians during the fighting in the North Caucasus, and left, Nazi soldiers passing some of the blazing oilfields in the neighbourhood of Maikop

CANADIANS LAND
AT DIEPPE

19 AUGUST, 1942

The biggest combined operations carried out on the Continent since the evacuation of Dunkirk took place on 19 August, when a large force, consisting mainly of Canadians, carried out a daring daylight landing at Dieppe and remained on French soil for nine hours before withdrawing. Officially described as a "reconnaissance in force," its objects were: (1) to test the defences of what was known to be a strongly fortified part of the enemy coast; (2) the destruction of German batteries and an important radiolocation station; and (3) the capture of prisoners for interrogation. Escorted by units of the Royal Navy, the force passed safely through the enemy minefields and landed according to schedule, at 4.50 a.m., on six selected beaches in the Dieppe area. At Varengeville, 4½ miles west of Dieppe, a Commando force succeeded in destroying an enemy 6-in. gun battery of howitzers, but at Berneval, 4½ miles east of Dieppe, a chance encounter with enemy E-boats and flak ships caused an initial set-back. Although landings were later made here, the enemy coastal guns were never silenced, and hindered the attackers on the central beaches throughout the operation. In the centre, at Pourville and Puys, tanks were landed from special landing craft, and Canadian troops, with tanks in support, fought their way into the centre of the town, where fierce fighting raged round the Casino. All the objectives of the raid were attained, and the withdrawal was carried out only six minutes after the scheduled time. All the tanks were blown up before re-embarkation. Throughout the day the Royal Navy supported the land operations by keeping up a constant bombardment of the enemy shore positions, and despite heavy retaliatory fire from German shore batteries only one ship, the destroyer H.M.S. "Berkeley," was lost. Operational commands of the R.A.F., as well as Canadian, New Zealand, Polish, Czech, Belgian, Fighting French and Norwegian squadrons provided air cover for the attack, and Flying Fortresses of the U.S. Army Air Corps made a high-level raid on the enemy airfield at Abbeville. The Germans called up air reinforcements from all parts of Occupied France, Belgium and Holland, but many of these were engaged and broken up by Allied airmen before they reached the scene of the operations. The picture shows British landing craft approaching Dieppe, where a fierce barrage is being put up by enemy batteries.

SUCCESS OF THE DIEPPE RAID. Throughout the Dieppe raid an extensive air umbrella provided support for the ground forces, and during the day, air fighting developed on a scale not seen since the Battle of Britain. In spite of the fact that the Allied airmen were operating over enemy territory, they shot down ninety-one aircraft for certain and damaged and probably destroyed twice that number. The Allies lost ninety-eight aircraft. The Germans tried to create the impression that the raid had been a full scale attempt at invasion, but this had been foreseen and forestalled by a B.B.C. broadcast to the French people during the early stages of the operation,

which urged them to avoid all action that would compromise their safety and told them that no invasion was contemplated. Canadians, who formed five-sixths of the attacking force, sustained casualties amounting to 3,350 men made up of 170 dead, 633 wounded, and 2,547 missing. The pictures show: left, above, a burning British landing craft and two Churchill tanks on the shore at Dieppe and below, a close-up view of a British tank whose tractor has been torn off. Some of the British airmen who took part in the operation are seen above, right, and below, some of the members of the attacking force are seen at a British port on their return.

FIGHTING IN THE DON ELBOW.   On 18 August the German armies driving towards Stalingrad from the north-west reached the Don south-east of Kletskaya, and five days later they succeeded in getting tanks and men across on to the east bank under cover of an aerial umbrella.   Farther south, the enemy drove a deep wedge into the Russian lines north-east of Kotelnikovo on the 24th thereby threatening Stalingrad from north and south.   The pictures show: above, Cossack cavalry gallantly charging to attack the enemy during the fighting on the Don, and below, an aer'al view of the Don elbow showing two out of three bridges completely destroyed.

Japanese set-back in New Guinea

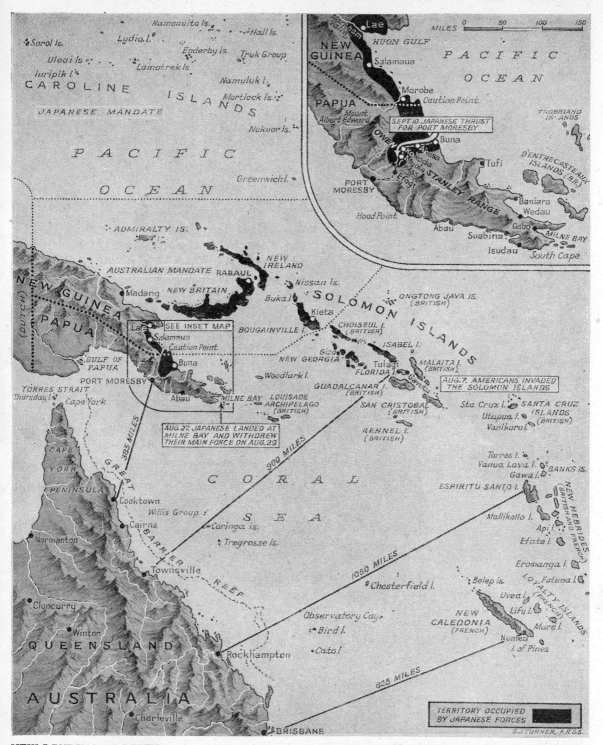

NEW LANDING IN PAPUA. In an effort to by-pass the Owen Stanley Mountains and capture Port Moresby, as well as to obtain an advance base for the recapture of their lost positions in the Solomons, Japanese troops landed at Milne Bay, Papua, on 27 August. Allied aircraft and Australian troops were waiting, unknown to the enemy, and inflicted such severe losses on his forces that the bulk of them were withdrawn on the 29th. The map, specially drawn for this book by S. J. Turner, F.R.G.S., shows the main centres of fighting in this area.

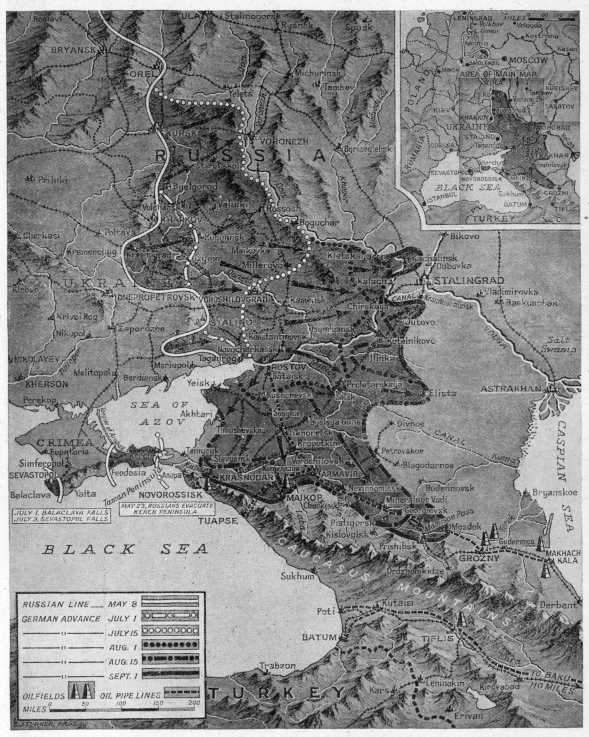

GERMAN ADVANCE IN RUSSIA. After their advance near Kotelnikovo on 24 August, both sides threw large numbers of reserves into the battle and fighting on a large scale developed along the whole front before Stalingrad. The Russians ceaselessly battered at the deep wedges the enemy had driven into their lines north and south of the city, but although they inflicted enormous losses on the enemy they were unable to bring him to a halt. The map shows the position on the Don and Caucasus fronts as the third year of war drew to an eventful end.

RENEWED FIGHTING IN EGYPT. On 31 August the Afrika Korps launched an attack on the British positions near Mt. Hemeimat. They were immediately engaged, and British bombers subjected them to a withering non-stop air attack. Although the enemy penetrated the British minefields at a few points, he was unable to pierce the defences, and on 2 September he retired nine miles. The pictures show: above, a U.S.-built tank travelling at speed near Mt. Hemeimat, and below, a patrol sheltering from shell fire near Mt. Hemeimat.

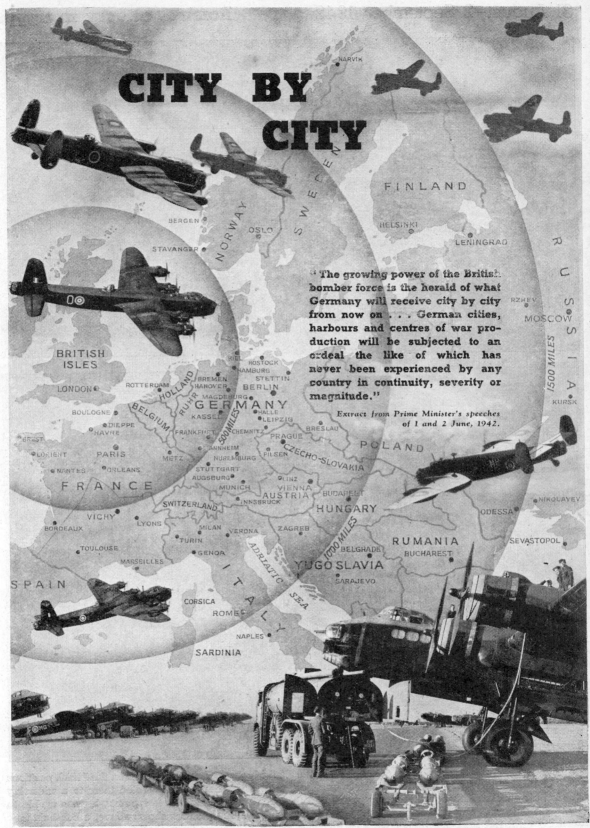

CITY BY CITY

"The growing power of the British bomber force is the herald of what Germany will receive city by city from now on . . . German cities, harbours and centres of war production will be subjected to an ordeal the like of which has never been experienced by any country in continuity, severity or magnitude."

Extract from Prime Minister's speeches of 1 and 2 June, 1942.

Printed by Odhams (Watford) Ltd., Watford. S. 143